A Serrated Edge

A Brief Defense of Biblical Satire
and Trinitarian Skylarking

Douglas Wilson

canonpress
Moscow, Idaho

Published by Canon Press
P.O. Box 8729, Moscow, ID 83843
800–488–2034 | www.canonpress.com

Cover design by Paige Atwood.
Interior design by Jared Miller.

Printed in the United States of America.

Library of Congress Cataloging-in-Publication Data

Wilson, Douglas,
  A serrated edge : a brief defense of biblical satire and
trinitarian skylarking / by Douglas Wilson.
     p. cm.
     Includes index.
  ISBN-13: 978-1-59128-010-1 (pbk.)
  ISBN-10: 1-59128-010-9 (pbk.)
  1. Satire—Religious aspects—Christianity. 2. Satire in the
     Bible. I. Title.
  BR115.S26W55 2003
  230'.044—dc21
                        2002154048

10 11 12 13 14 15 16   9 8 7 6 5 4 3

CONTENTS

Preface   7

1. Satiric Bite   11
2. The Meaning of Arrogance   19
3. The Satire of Jesus   29
4. Old Testament Satire and Jabs   47
5. The Language of Paul   61
6. Dearlybelovedism   69
7. ModEvism   77
8. Spurgeon the Magnificent   85
9. Objections   93
10. The Goal of Giving Offense   101
11. Apathetic Sanctity   111
12. Tender Mercies   115

Appendix: Seductive Disrespect
by Douglas Jones   121

Scripture Index   126

This book is for Rachel, who is one
of our graces in submissive wit.

Whatever is funny is
subversive, every joke is
ultimately a custard pie.
George Orwell

Absurdity is always a
serious art.
G.K. Chesterton

PREFACE
Prolegomena to Any Future Big Words

This small book may be considered as a work of exhortation. As I say this, I am mindful of Ambrose Bierce's definition of this most virtuous activity. "Exhort, v.t. In religious affairs, to put the conscience of another upon the spit and roast it to a nut-brown discomfort."

So perhaps I should say this is a work of *defensive* exhortation. As the editor of the magazine entitled *Credenda/Agenda*, I am often asked something along the lines of, "What gives?" Behind such penetrating questions is the common assumption that the foibles of modern evangelicalism are treated, within our pages, with a less than perfect tenderness. This causes distress in some quarters, glee in others, and FAQs for the editors.

The assumptions behind such questions are fairly widespread, *fairly* here meaning "kind of" and not "with considerable justice." From time to time, some folks will make their way out to Moscow, Idaho, which is the magazine's point of origin, in order to visit us. Prior to their arrival, their only knowledge of the place comes from the pages of our magazine. And after a short time here, they frequently discover that the people they meet who are associated with the magazine are, well, pleasant, and this disorients them. Not what they thought was on the menu.

A story not related to *Credenda* still illustrates the principles involved quite nicely. My wife was once in conversation with a woman she did not really know, and, as the conversation developed, the lights began to go on in the other woman's head. She then asked if my wife was married to Douglas Wilson. When Nancy confessed that this was in fact the case, the woman she was talking to expressed herself well. "But you seem so *nice!*"

Our investigations reveal that the austere world of black and white careful analysis, epistemological invective, doctrinal sarcasm, and eschatological jihad has obscured our sunny selves from public view. This is not necessarily a bad thing because our sunny selves can also take some getting used to. But we still thought a small book was in order. In the pages of *Credenda*, we are too busy doing what we do to explain it fully, but at some point an explanation is still called for. So here is a slim volume to put right next to that ever-growing *Hardy Boys in the Apocalypse* series by LaHaye and Jenkins. Call it our *apologia* for not apologizing.

Who will read this modest effort? Well, for starters, a lot of people initially got on our mailing list because some zealous reformer in their family added his whole Christmas card list, and the said reformer is now in some trouble with his Aunt Henrietta, a soft-spoken amillennial Lutheran. So zealous name-adders should read this, if only to have something to say at the next tense family get-together at Thanksgiving.

And then there is the curious fellow who likes what we are doing but still feels guilty about it. He laughs at most of the jabs but then starts violently, comes to himself, and shakes his head quietly. *Tsk.* Guilt-free polemics is a whole new concept, and he might go for it if a biblical case is made for it.

Another potential reader is the ammo-gatherer. He is trying to come up with a platonic form letter to the editor, one that will shut us up for good, and you know, it might.

But at the end of the day, even if customers do not start clogging up Canon Press's order lines, we still have the option of sending the book out as a gift to those who support the magazine financially. This is the preaching to the choir angle, but this cliche overlooks the fact that choirs sometimes need preaching to.

If I can stay on track, the book will be organized around two basic themes. Objections to our *joie de vivre* can be divided into two general categories. The first is that what we are doing is unkind, and therefore unbiblical. The second is that what we are doing is counterproductive, that we are chasing people away from our position. Our response to these objections could be summarized in a two-fold fashion, reading from left to right as *Oh yeah?* and *Nuh uh.* But this requires further development.

ONE

Satiric Bite

There is a marked difference between a gun in a gun cabinet and that same gun being employed on the field of battle. A man could know all about a particular make of gun but still lose his composure when it is pointed at him. In a similar way, satire can be quite delightful if the objects of the attack have been dead for centuries, but, as it turns out, contemporary satire is a different matter.

For various reasons, satire is studied today as something of a museum piece, in much the same way that a military historian might analyze a crossbow. The learned and respectable among us have agreed to abandon the use of satire, leaving this particular form of abuse to the buffooneries of late night comedians. Our academicized scholars have gravitated to *respectable* discourse, along with other forms of surrender.

This does not mean we have no knowledge of literary and learned satire. The names Swift, Erasmus, and Juvenal come to mind. But who does this kind of thing any more? Can anyone name a respectable academic journal where one theologian might dismiss another as a barking dog? Literary academics have studied satire as a literary genre, and they have described it well. Moreover, to their credit they have even seen that this genre is pervasive throughout Scripture, so much so that the Bible can actually be described as relying heavily on satire. "Satire is prominent in the biblical narrative, where wholly idealized characters are a rarity and deficient or immoral human behavior is the staple."[1]

Satire treats the foibles of sinners with a less than perfect tenderness. "Satire is the exposure of human vice or folly through rebuke or ridicule. . . . It might consist of an entire book (e.g., Amos), or it can be as small as an individual 'proverb.'"[2] But nevertheless, if a Christian employs satire today, he is almost immediately called to account for his "unbiblical" behavior. There are many explanations for this, and it is hoped that this small book will address the more important of them. But we should begin by noting the true *oddness* of our position. Suppose a man were to refer to certain respected theologians dismissively as having graduated from Bag of Snakes Seminary. He would instantly be upbraided for his un-Christlike behavior. Unfortunately for the one delivering the rebuke, it was discovered shortly thereafter that the speaker was Christ (Mt. 23:33).

According to literary analysis, satire consists of four basic elements. There is, in the first place, an object of attack, which

---

1. Ryken, Wilhoit, Longman, eds. *Dictionary of Biblical Imagery* (Downers Grove: InterVarsity Press, 1998), 762.
2. Ibid.

can be specific or general, but which is more likely to be particular, concrete, and very specific. The reason for an attack at all is usually a specific problem or group, and if an attack is too general, then it will tend to miss the target. And so this is why the prophet Jeremiah attacked idolaters, the Lord Jesus attacked self-righteous Pharisees, the apostle Paul attacked Judaizers, Irenaeus attacked Gnostics, and Luther attacked the papists. This does not mean that only one legitimate target exists at a given point in time, but usually a man is called by his gifts and circumstances to fight one battle at a time. There were idolaters around during the lifetime of Irenaeus but he still had it out with the Gnostics. In my writing, the object of attack has usually been what I call *modern evangelicalism*. I bring this up not to introduce a little autobiographical interest but rather to make an important connection. The reason for writing this small book is to give an answer to those who are distressed or concerned over such tactics, and consequently it is necessary to give a specific defense of these specific attacks. For now it should suffice to say that modern evangelicalism (not historic evangelicalism) is represented by what one president called the axis of treacle—*Christianity Today*, the Christian Booksellers Association, Wheaton College and its environs, Colorado Springs and its environs, Thomas Kinkade, and Jerry B. Jenkins.

The second characteristic of satire is the satiric vehicle. This is usually some kind of story, descriptive narrative, or word picture. A person might write a novel or short story in order to lay waste to a particular target, or he might include a brief description of his target in the course of doing something else. Tom Wolfe's *Bonfire of the Vanities* is a book-length demolition job of various social strata in New York City, from Wall Street high flyers to racial agitators. The prophet Isaiah delivers a devastating aside in his description of the daughters of Zion strutting their stuff down at the mall (Is.3:16–26). At the same time, the description might be as brief as a single potent metaphor. Solomon does this when he says that a beautiful woman without discretion is like putting lipstick on a camel or something (Prov. 11:22).

The third characteristic of satire concerns its tone, which can be divided into two basic categories. Literary scholars have named these approaches after the two Roman satirists who embody them. "Horatian satire (named after Horace) is light, urbane and subtle."[3] This form of satire has a deft touch and relies on a knowing or discerning audience. One biblical master of this was Luke. If a reader is not paying attention, the satiric element can be entirely missed. For example, Luke delivers a jab at the philosophy department at the University of Athens. All the learned johnnies there "spent their time in nothing else, but either to tell, or to hear some new thing" (Acts 17:21).

On another occasion, Luke reports in a very dry manner about how Sosthenes was getting beat up outside the courthouse. But inside, Judge Gallio remained supremely indifferent. "And Gallio cared for none of those things" (Acts 18:17). Luke makes fun of the debating skills exhibited by a rioting crowd. "But when they knew that he was a Jew, all with one voice about the space of two hours cried out, Great is Diana of the Ephesians" (Acts 19:34). Something similar happened

3. Ibid.

when Paul got to an unacceptable part of his speech to a crowd. "And as they cried out, and cast off their clothes, and threw dust into the air" (Acts 22:23). In none of these instances does Luke use a heavy hand, but in all of them we find out what he thought, and what his chuckle probably sounded like.

But still there are times when it is necessary to set aside the surgeon's scalpel and pick up a Louisville Slugger. "Juvenalian satire (named after Juvenal) is biting, bitter and angry, as epitomized by the book of Amos and Jesus' oratory against the Pharisees in Matthew 23."[4] This is a "take no prisoners" approach, and the difference between the two tones is the difference between needling and cudgeling. "Hear this word, ye kine of Bashan, that are in the mountain of Samaria, which oppress the poor, which crush the needy, which say to their masters, Bring, and let us drink" (Amos 4:1). This quotation from the Authorized Version can be misleading—*kine* means cows—and when we also take into account our tendency to cover all quotations from Scripture with three layers of our high gloss holyspeak varnish, it is not surprising that we miss what Amos does here, and how potent his insult actually is. Picture the prophet ministering in Texas among the monied interests of big oil there, and imagine what would happen when he started talking about the Heifers of Houston in his after-dinner speech. "Yeah, you. With bangly earrings the size of softballs."

The Juvenalian approach can be harsh or buoyant. When Jesus describes His adversaries as vipers, the tone is a straightforward denunciation. But if someone were to describe a bureaucrat

4. Ibid.

as one asleep at his desk so long that one side of his head was flat, this would be Juvenalian also—the point being most unsubtle—and funnier than simple denunciations like "lazy bureaucrat." Jesus uses both forms of Juvenalian satire. For example, He calls His opponents whited sepulchers, which is kind of harsh and critical, and He also says they like to strain minnows out of their coffee while missing the sea lion in there, which is kind of funny.

In the satire of a magazine like *Credenda*, we have tried to be what might be called jolly Juvenalians. This is not done because the other tones are objectionable, or because we believe ourselves to be particularly good at it, but simply because this has suited our goals and personalities better. As mentioned above, the Scriptures are thoroughly satiric. This being the case, it is not surprising that the Bible contains examples of the various kinds of satiric tone. We do not find a divine requirement for a "one size fits all" approach, but one approach may suit a particular set of editorial personalities better than another.

And last, satire requires a norm, which for biblical satire is the character of God as revealed in the Scriptures. There is always a sense that the satirist knows what "ought to be." He does not talk about it *directly* a great deal, but he assumes it constantly. When Pharisees are rebuked for hypocrisy, the decency of honesty is assumed. When they are mocked for not knowing that gold has no power to sanctify the altar, the duty of not inverting perspective is assumed (Is. 5:20). When Jesus talked about how the Pharisees would diligently tithe out of their spice rack while forgetting details like mercy and justice, He was assuming the honesty of proportionality.

Now the biblical norm has two functions in our discussion. The first is the norm of overt example, which has been discussed briefly here. But the second aspect of this is the normativity of the Trinitarian worldview. To simplify, in defending satire, it should be enough that the Scriptures contain massive amounts of it. But defenders of modern satire often find (as I have) that the simple fact that the Bible contains such language is by itself entirely unconvincing. And this is because certain non-Christian assumptions have come to dominate how we read the Bible.

When Jesus looked on the rich, young ruler and loved him, it is very easy for us to say that we should be loving as He was. When preachers make such applications, no one thinks anything of it. But when Jesus looked on the rich, old rulers and insulted them, why do we tend to assume that this is never, *ever* to be imitated? It is conceivable that such a division is defensible, but why does it never have to be defended? Some might say (and do say) that we are not Jesus, and so we do not have the wisdom to insult properly. Fine. So why then do we have the wisdom to *love* properly? Can't we screw that up too?

Instead of seeking to learn our paradigms of behavior from the Scriptures, we tend to bring our assumptions, learned elsewhere and from others, and view the Scriptures through those assumptions. This is not a superficial problem; it goes down to the bone. The prophets, the apostles and our Lord Jesus all exhibit a vast array of verbal behavior, including tenderness, love, insults, jokes, anger, and more. What standard do we use to sort this material out?

When this standard is a scriptural one, the same range of expression will be found in those who imitate the Scriptures, and that range will exhibit scriptural proportions. But when the standard is nonscriptural, and has excluded a certain type of expression as being *a priori* un-Christlike, it then will not matter how many passages are cited which show Christ being un-Christlike. And at that point we may take a jibe from Christ's arsenal and say that wisdom is vindicated by her children.

TWO

The Meaning of Arrogance

Far from being urbane and civilized, respectable (and widely respected) academic discourse on the part of evangelicals in the realm of basic theological debates is actually a manifestation of spiritual surrender. The assumption that collegiality is owed in *all* debates is an assumption based on widespread but false notions of neutrality, and since neutrality is impossible, acceptance of such assumptions is simply a tacit way of going over to the other side. The "other side" in this case is the view that the bonds of academic collegiality are deeper and more profound than the bonds created by baptism in the name of the Father, Son, and Holy Spirit.

The phrase *inescapable concept* points us back to the fundamental issues of life. For example, when we consider the "concept" of Deity, we see that it is "not whether, but which." It is not *whether* we will serve God, but rather *which* god we will serve. It is not whether we will impose morality through law, but rather which morality we will impose, and so on.

In the same way, God has divided the world between the seed of the woman and the seed of the serpent, and since that time ridicule has been inescapable. It is not *whether* we will ridicule a group, it is *which* group we will ridicule—and whether we will notice when we have done so. Whenever ridicule is applied from within a particular worldview to those outside it, that ridicule is almost always invisible to most of those within the ridiculing group. Satire, ridicule, and invective, however, are always immediately obvious to those outside the group that produced it.

To say that ridicule is necessary is not to say that every person in the world has to stand on street corners yelling at the passing motorists. It is not to say that everyone has to talk. In Paul's wonderful image, the body has different organs, there are different gifts. But everyone within the body is complicit in such activity, all the time. Some kind of antithesis is always manifest, everyone in the world lines up in terms of it, and in that act of lining up, one either ridicules the other side or accepts the ridicule delivered to the other side in their name and on their behalf. A man does not have to be a soldier to be protected by an army. And if he is not protected by an army, the time will quickly come when he will cease to be a nonsoldier, because he will be dead.

In the same way, everyone in the world receives the protections of a certain society or group. That group defends itself, necessarily, by means of ridicule, satire, and so forth, defining itself over against the other groups by these means. Of course, it is not required that every member of that society be a "combatant." But if he accepts his identification with that group, and is not seeking to subvert it, then he is complicit.

Those Christians in our culture who do not understand the inescapability of ridicule, and who have accepted the assurances that neutrality is possible, are constantly complaining about the injustices that are regularly perpetrated against them. In other words, since fair play between all groups is thought to be *possible*, then the lack of "fair play" is seen as an instance of the other team breaking the rules, rather than as a simple necessity given the nature of the case.

To illustrate this, in our culture today it is common to divide society into two groups—victims and oppressors. If someone falls into the category of an "oppressor," then he is fair game. If someone is a "victim," then to strike against him verbally is a hate crime. This is not a novelty; the only thing that is different (at any time) is how the two groups are defined. Every society has an orthodoxy (which is invisible to most adherents of it), and every society has its heretics, those who challenge that orthodoxy. The heretics may be taunted and assaulted verbally (and at times, physically). In times of transition, when one orthodoxy is being supplanted by another, there is usually a pretence of neutrality until the new orthodoxy consolidates its forces—and its abilities to enforce the new codes.

Christians who do not understand what is going on see themselves as victims of foul play within this new order. But according to the definitions of the new orthodoxy, biblical Christianity is in the oppressor category—the tyrant which must be overthrown. "Why won't you let us be the victims?" Christians complain. "Because you are *not*," comes the reply. By definition.

Older forms of insult (which presupposed an out-of-date orthodoxy) are highly offensive to us today. But recently minted forms of insult (which reflect the reigning orthodoxy) are not seen as such at all. In our culture today, protection of authorized victim status is the reigning orthodoxy. Again, it is not *whether* there is an orthodoxy, it is which orthodoxy there is.

This is because every orthodoxy protects its sacred things with blasphemy laws. Because our culture likes to keep up its secularist pretense, we do not use the term *orthodoxy* or *blasphemy*. But we do have politically correct thought, and we do have laws against hate speech. Furthermore, and related to this, every established orthodoxy maintains the definitions of arrogance, and this brings us to our point—a defense of biblical satire. Whenever someone uses satire against the current regime, among other things, he is invariably accused of arrogance. The orthodoxy is the keeper of the keys, and those keys include the definitions.

Allow me to drift into a couple of examples, one of them autobiographical. A number of years ago, the first book I wrote came out. This was an exciting moment for me, and one in which I discovered how typos, cleverly hidden before publication, become immediately and glaringly obvious upon publication. But I have digressed—typos are not the central point. Someone in our church gave a copy of this book to a relative who was from another theological tradition entirely. Some time later, this person told me that the relative had thought the book "arrogant." This distressed me, and I went back to the book and opened it up. There in the foreword, just like the typos, was a small forest of the first person personal pronoun *I*. Big as life—*I, I, I*. Of course I was humiliated and told my friend to tell the relative that he had a point, and that I was sorry. But she said something like, "Oh, no. That's not why he thought it was arrogant. It was the *rest* of the book, where you quoted from the Bible all the time."

In other words, he had no problem with me talking about *me*. That was humble enough. But when I presumed to say what God had revealed—*that* was arrogant. But notice how different definitions of arrogance are at work here. There is no neutrality anywhere, especially in the realm of defining what constitutes arrogance and what does not.

We see the same thing in the conflict between biblical and modern theories of preaching. The biblical preacher is a herald, a steward. He has been entrusted to declare something that would have been true if he had never been born. He is to preach it with a strong view of his own ultimate irrelevance. He is to get into the pulpit and say, "Thus says the Lord . . . ." And to the modern world, this is insufferable arrogance.

In stark contrast with this, a modern pretty boy preacher— excuse me, a pretty boy communicator—gets up front and can talk about *himself* the entire time he is there. He is open, transparent, honest, and emotionally approachable. He is humble, or so it is thought. The evidence? He is humble because he talked about himself *a lot*. And the other one, the insufferable one, *he* must think he has a personal pipeline to God. He must think that God wrote a book or something . . . wait.

The apostle Paul says, "For we preach not ourselves, but Christ Jesus the Lord; and ourselves your servants for Jesus' sake" (2 Cor. 4:5). In the biblical pattern, arrogance preaches self while humility preaches Christ. In the modern world, we see how the reality of our inescapable concept takes over. In order to revolt against the biblical pattern, it is necessary to reverse these values. It is not possible to go off to a neutral zone where these categories do not apply. This basic divide must either be *embraced* or *reversed*. So in the brave new world, arrogance preaches Christ and humility talks about self.

Every charge of arrogance always *presupposes a standard*. The question for us must always be whether or not that standard is a Trinitarian standard derived from the Scriptures. If it is not, then it is a humanistic standard, derived from hostility to the Trinitarian standards of Scripture.

One of the greatest problems in the Church today is that we do not understand that for those who hate God, love for God is arrogance. For those who love God, hatred of God is arrogance. These are not what we may call reconcilable definitions. The nonnegotiable standard is the standard given to us by Scripture. When we commit ourselves to this standard, *a priori*, and are determined to resist all ungodly attempts to define arrogance, a strange thing happens. Much of what we have previously assumed as arrogant is suddenly seen as humility, and vice versa. This brings us to the place where we can recognize that we had been seduced to an unbiblical definition of sin. And Isaiah pronounces a woe on those who call evil good, and good evil (Is. 5:20).

Now of course, we have to acknowledge that the orthodoxy required by the Bible does reject arrogance. As we have seen, *every* orthodoxy rejects arrogance. But the Scriptures reject the genuine arrogance of those who presume themselves wiser than God. And this would include those who pretend to embrace the standard of the Bible while at the same time undermining those standards—whether this is done by conservatives, moderates, or liberals does not matter. When Jesus had a couple of zealous disciples who wanted to rain down fire on a particular village, the Lord told them that they did not know "what spirit they were of" (Lk. 9:55–56). In a similar way, some "friends" of God really have been arrogant in how they fight the enemies of God. But they are arrogant because of how the Scriptures describe their behavior, and not because they have hurt the enemy's feelings.

Put another way, there are rebukes that must be delivered within the camp of the saints. And we must acknowledge that there are sins of arrogance that we must confess. But when we receive such rebukes, we must remember that those who deliver them are doing so on the basis of a standard. What standard is it? When they rebuke us for arrogance, are they being arrogant?

Arrogance *cannot* be defined as the necessary result of assuming yourself to be right and the other fellow wrong. For what would happen if we decided that someone else had succumbed to this temptation and was being arrogant? Should we go admonish him? If we do so, are we assuming that we are right and he is wrong?

Arrogance is the sin of assuming yourself to be in the right without warrant from the Word of God. In other words, we must make our standard explicit, or we will run ourselves into hopeless contradictions. This is because everyone in the world always believes that he is right. This is part of the human condition.

In other words, I always believe that I am right. This is not the same thing as believing that I am always right. I know that

I have often been wrong. Nevertheless, I, along with everyone else in the world, always believe (at the time the view is maintained) that I am right. No one ever said that he was convinced that thus and such was the case, but that he was "not" convinced that it was the case. So when someone comes to rebuke me for always thinking I am right, is he coming with this rebuke because he thinks he is *wrong* about it?

This problem of arrogance arises whenever we refuse to bring our views to the bar of Scripture to be corrected there. And if we are willing to be corrected there, it does not matter what the world thinks about it.

So when modern evangelicalism is handled somewhat critically or roughly, one of the common complaints or questions amounts to this—"Who do you think you are?" This is a variant of a question that comes up in Scripture frequently, which is, "By what authority do you do this?" Everyone understands that random acts of kindness, provided they stay within certain bounds, and are not overtly meddlesome, require little or no authority to perform. But verbal admonitions, rebukes, jabs and jokes are all at bottom authoritative acts. And this leads to the question—"Who died and left *you* king?" And since the answer to that question is not visible to the questioner, it is assumed that the satirist has simply taken it upon himself to make fun of other people, and what could be more arrogant than that?

Because the world is fallen, because it contains sin, it contains competing authorities. If God were the only authority then there would be no sin. Sin or rebellion consists in the first place of setting up a competing authority to the authority of God. This is how sin entered in the first place—the serpent challenged the authority of God's Word. He did this in the first place by questioning the boundaries of that Word and ended his temptation of the woman by challenging that Word directly. "You shall not die" (Gen. 3:4).

Arrogance, defined biblically, is the practice of challenging the will of the triune God. Every aspiring idol, precisely because it is aspiring to replace the triune God, must seek (however unsuccessfully) to take on the same attributes. This means that idols try to define arrogance in the same way. Arrogance is that which challenges the god who seeks to reign.

This means that when modern evangelicalism has compromised fatally with the idols of the age (which it most certainly has), and when someone points it out in a way that cannot be ignored, the basic defense of the idolatry is to attack the critic as one who is arrogant.

Now of course, as already noted, it is possible for an orthodox Trinitarian to attack unbelief in a way that really is arrogant. But it is arrogant because the Trinitarian is being inconsistent with what the *Scriptures* require of him. He is orthodox in one way, but disobedient in another. Suppose he attacks some form of unbelief, but he does so filled with a spirit of malice and selfish hatred. This is arrogant, because he is setting himself up as a defender of God who is not bound to conduct himself the way that God commands.

But an attack on unbelief is never arrogant simply because unbelievers claim that it is arrogant. Nor is it arrogant because compromised believers think that such an attack is arrogant. In short, arrogance is never determined by examining the results of a survey or poll. The issue, always, is the authority of the Word of God.

And this is why the basic question about arrogance is the same in every discussion of every issue—Who is God? And if He has spoken, dare we challenge that Word?

THREE

The Satire of Jesus

One of the frequent charges made against this kind of satire is that it is "unfair" to the recipients. In logical argumentation, this is called the straw man fallacy. You fashion an opponent more to your liking, one easier to take apart, and then you proceed to do so. But there is a legitimate polemic that is often mistaken for this fallacy—when genuine straw men are accurately identified as such. This is where the folly of the adversary is clearly seen, identified as folly, and then is highlighted *and thereby refuted* through exaggeration and caricature. Before we start to protest against this style of argument, however, we need to note that it was Christ's favorite form. He did this kind of thing all the time. "The most characteristic form of Jesus' humor was the preposterous exaggeration."[1]

But before considering Christ's hard-hitting style, we should begin by noting that He was skilled in the milder Horatian

---

1. Ryken, *Biblical Imagery*, 410.

approach. While His preferred form is the Agent Orange approach, Christ is also capable of a much milder form of irony. In other words, He is not always Juvenalian. Jesus answered them, "Many good works have I showed you from my Father; for which of those works do ye stone me?" (Jn. 10:32) Which healing of which leper brought on this particular attempt to apply the death penalty? And when He was setting His face to go to Jerusalem He said, "Nevertheless I must walk today, and tomorrow, and the day following: for it cannot be that a prophet perish out of Jerusalem" (Lk. 13:33). Christ had thought about it, but had a hard time thinking of any righteous prophet who had not met a bloody end at the hands of God's chosen people. This is obviously a mild jab.

And His response to a supposed threat from Herod was hardly over the top—but it was still there. "The same day there came certain of the Pharisees, saying unto him, Get thee out, and depart hence: for Herod will kill thee. And he said unto them, Go ye, and tell that fox, Behold, I cast out devils, and I do cures today and tomorrow, and the third day I shall be perfected" (Lk. 13:31–32). Go tell the fox he has been outfoxed. This kind of humor is seen in how He nicknamed Peter (Mt. 16:16–18). Just as we might name a huge man Slim, Jesus took His most impetuous disciple and named him the Rock.

But as indicated earlier, Jesus was really in His element when it came to flamboyant verbal display.

> Then said Jesus unto his disciples, Verily I say unto you, That a rich man shall hardly enter into the kingdom of heaven. And again I say unto you, It is easier for a camel to go through the eye of a needle, than for a rich man

to enter into the kingdom of God. (Mt. 19:23–24; Mk. 10:25; Lk. 18:25)

It is important to emphasize (yet again) that we have emptied such hilarious comparisons of their force because we have bought into a false notion of holiness concerning them. Since Jesus is the Son of God, we say, and since this is the *Bible*, we say, there can be nothing here to make us laugh out loud. Nothing, that is, except for the preposterous mental image that Jesus paints, and which we, for the sake of maintaining our taxidermified pieties, dutifully ignore. And so it is that we hear edifying interpretations about camels getting down on their knees in order to get through the needle gate! And actually, *that* interpretation is a pretty funny one in its own right—camels at prayer and all—but the thundering boredoms of conventional piety prevent anyone from getting the new joke. So let us try the same thing, only with a twist. "It is easier for a '72 Ford pickup to go through the tailpipe of a Toyota, than for a rich man to enter into the kingdom of God." Or something.

Judge not, that ye be not judged. For with what judgment ye judge, ye shall be judged: and with what measure ye mete, it shall be measured to you again. And why beholdest thou the mote that is in thy brother's eye, but considerest not the beam that is in thine own eye? Or how wilt thou say to thy brother, Let me pull out the mote out of thine eye; and, behold, a beam *is* in thine own eye? Thou hypocrite, first cast out the beam out of thine own eye; and then shalt thou see clearly to cast out the mote out of thy brother's eye. Give not that which is holy unto the dogs, neither cast ye your pearls before swine, lest they trample them under their feet, and turn again and rend you. (Mt. 7:1–6; cf. Lk. 6:41)

This famous passage has two ludicrous images. A man who tries to correct his brother, with a standard that he himself does not follow, is guilty of a very serious sin indeed. Jesus identifies that sin for us here—it is hypocrisy—but the fact that it is a serious sin does not keep Him from making fun of it. A self-important man has undertaken amateur ophthalmology in order to get a speck off his neighbor's contact lens when he has managed to get a railroad tie gummed onto his own. When the laughter dies down, what further refutation is necessary?

The second image has someone feeding the dogs out in the kennels off his wife's best wedding china, and then, for good measure, pitching the contents of the jewelry case over the rail into the pigsty. And it probably seemed like a good idea to him at the time.

Jesus has not engaged in the serious arguments that such people might bring forward. Is He therefore guilty of the straw man fallacy? No, because Scripture is the final authority, which means that appealing to the straw man fallacy is sometimes a fallacy. But the question remains; is this how *they* would represent what they are doing? No, but that doesn't matter. Jesus is not giving His theological opponents a "fair" shake. "Let them alone: they be blind leaders of the blind. And if the blind lead the blind, both shall fall into the ditch" (Mt. 15:14; Lk. 6:39).

And this leads to a very important point about the biblical approach to polemics. Collisions between light and darkness do not occur on the proverbial "level playing field." When we attend a football game, we expect the contest to be even-handed. We want the teams to change directions to equalize wind and sun-in-your-eye problems. We want the refs to identify clipping by the same standard regardless of what color uniform was involved. We want both teams to have to move the ball ten yards for a first down; we do not want the game rigged so that the home team only has to get five yards. In short, at a football game, we want a "level playing field."

But this is not the case in a verbal clash between Christ and the Pharisees. In the passage noted above, He gets to call them blind guides for the blind—because they are. *They* do not get to call Him a blind guide, because they are blind and don't know. The same principle arises in conflicts two thousand years after the closure of the canon. A minister of the gospel has to rebuke with all authority (Tit. 2:15), and if he is young, he should let no one despise his youth (1 Tim. 4:12). He should have a sense of the dignity of his office, and, insofar as the cause of the gospel is wrapped up in his person, he must defend his person (2 Cor. 11:5–15). And when he identifies his opponents as, say, vipers, and then objects when they identify him in the same way, *he is not being inconsistent*. But the accusation is quickly brought—"He can dish it out, but he can't take it." The assumption of inconsistency in this shows how much unbiblical presuppositions underlie our debates on all these things. Right? Wrong? These are curious words. We have assumed that full knowledge of the right is not possible, and this being the case, we have turned debates into a form of entertainment, like a football game. And that is why we insist on a level playing field. We do this, and to the extent we do it, we are unbelievers.

Jesus loved to appeal to outlandish images that we, through long and wrong usage, have prettified. "That's a great restoration job on this '57 Chevy," He says. "But why did you move the headlights into the trunk?" (Mk. 4:21). Of course, the fellow at work who was a little embarrassed about his Christian faith would not have described his behavior in such a way—he would have described it in a much more dignified way. But the biblical descriptions of these things are out on the skinny branches.

Speaking of branches, Jesus teaches us that grapefruits don't grow on the rosebush. "Ye shall know them by their fruits. Do men gather grapes of thorns, or figs of thistles?" (Mt. 7:16; Lk. 6:44). He gives us the picture of dead undertakers. "But Jesus said unto him, Follow me; and let the dead bury their dead" (Mt. 8:22; cf. Lk. 9:60). One of the great elements in humor is that of incongruity, and when it comes to portraying incongruities, Jesus is a master. But He does not do this because He likes to tell jokes. He uses this form of humor as a polemical weapon. He uses it in controversy.

One time the Lord compared the forgiving of a million-dollar debt for a man who then refused to forgive another man who had failed to pay back a quarter. "But the same servant went out, and found one of his fellowservants, which owed him an hundred pence: and he laid hands on him, and took him by the throat, saying, Pay me that thou owest" (Mt. 18:28). In much of Christ's teaching, we have this consistent element of righteous caricature.

The best example of this is found in Matthew 23, the most extended polemic in the New Testament. Not only is the caricature righteous in this chapter, it can also fairly be described as slashing. In this passage, we have the verbal equivalent of the cleansing of the Temple. When He cleansed the Temple, Jesus had made a whip of cords and driven the livestock out of the court of the Gentiles. In this place He makes a whip of words and drives the stubborn bovine theologians before Him.

> Then spake Jesus to the multitude, and to his disciples, saying, The scribes and the Pharisees sit in Moses' seat: All therefore whatsoever they bid you observe, that observe and do; but do not ye after their works: for they say, and do not. For they bind heavy burdens and grievous to be borne, and lay them on men's shoulders; but they themselves will not move them with one of their fingers. (vv. 1–4)

These people love work—they could watch it all day. They love cooking up spiritual things for other people to do. It reminds me of Ambrose Bierce's definition of a Christian— someone who believes that the New Testament is a divinely-inspired book, admirably suited to the spiritual needs of his neighbor. Was Jesus generalizing? Of course. Were there Pharisees who were *not* hypocrites? Of course. Did this stop Jesus from letting the whole group have it? Of course not. In fact, we might go so far as to define a good Pharisee as one who acknowledged the justice of Christ's generalizations.

In my frequent attacks on modern evangelicals, do I acknowledge that such attacks are generalizations? Of course. Do I know that there are contemporary evangelicals out there who have a spiritual backbone? Of course. Is this going to slow me down? Of course not. Modern evangelicalism, taken as a whole, is a wretched, money-grubbing business that has sold its soul for a market share. Why should we hold back the charge because there are some honest evangelicals who acknowledge that the charge is true? Holding back would make liars out of them.

> But all their works they do for to be seen of men: they make broad their phylacteries, and enlarge the borders of their garments, and love the uppermost rooms at feasts, and the chief seats in the synagogues. (vv. 5–6)

Their Bibles are more underlined than other people's. They showboat their way up to the stage where the pulpit used to be, and caper prettily back down again. They are *most* telegenic, and their charisma oozes over the airwaves. Their hair is more naturally blow-dried than their spiritual competitors. They provide spiritual counsel to the president in times of crisis. These are the kind of people who have written more books than they have read, and when such a book comes out it is sure to have a *large* photo of them on the back of the flyleaf.

And they like being called *doctor*.

> And greetings in the markets, and to be called of men, Rabbi, Rabbi. But be not ye called Rabbi: for one is your Master, even Christ; and all ye are brethren. And call no man your father upon the earth: for one is your Father, which is in heaven. Neither be ye called masters: for one is your Master, even Christ. But he that is greatest among you shall be your servant. And whosoever

shall exalt himself shall be abased; and he that shall humble himself shall be exalted. (vv. 7–12)

In the old days, this trick had to be accomplished by means of respectful titles like the "Rev." But nowadays, in these egalitarian times, the attitude of spiritual conceit has had to be a little more creative, and a pastor shows his prowess in humility by asking people to call him Joe. Behind the scenes he is a fierce, hard-driving CEO, and reads those CEO magazines, and acts like a CEO on airplanes, right down to ogling the flight attendants in first class. But out in front of the congregation, sitting on that stool, fitted out in a Mr. Rogers cardigan, he is open, transparent, and shares the struggles of his heart—the struggles of a simple guy . . . named Joe. He is about as deep as a wet spot on the pavement.

These men opposed by Christ played the role of dog in the manger well. They were not about to eat the food there, and they would not let anyone else approach.

But woe unto you, scribes and Pharisees, hypocrites! for ye shut up the kingdom of heaven against men: for ye neither go in yourselves, neither suffer ye them that are entering to go in. (v. 13; cf. Lk. 11:52)

It is amazing that we have been talking about religious hypocrisy for so long and have not really gotten into the greed issues. But here they are, right on schedule. "Woe unto you, scribes and Pharisees, hypocrites! for ye devour widows' houses, and for a pretence make long prayer: therefore ye shall receive the greater damnation" (Mt. 23:14). High profile piety and high levels of greed have been often seen together at a cheap motel late at night.

And the next taunt (for that is what these are) goes right to the heart of modern evangelicalism, in which evangelistic zeal excuses just about anything. But, the Lord points out, you can only export what you are manufacturing. If you have a stupid religion, then evangelistic zeal just gets you more of it. If you have rank hypocrisy, then why should we want to get that planted in the Third World? "Woe unto you, scribes and Pharisees, hypocrites! for ye compass sea and land to make one proselyte, and when he is made, ye make him twofold more the child of hell than yourselves" (v. 15).

Religious fools have the defining characteristic of being unable to follow a basic ethical argument. They *can* follow their own interests, however, and this is what they do. And Jesus gives their rationalizations the drubbing they deserve.

> Woe unto you, ye blind guides, which say, Whosoever shall swear by the temple, it is nothing; but whosoever shall swear by the gold of the temple, he is a debtor! Ye fools and blind: for whether is greater, the gold, or the temple that sanctifieth the gold? And, Whosoever shall swear by the altar, it is nothing; but whosoever sweareth by the gift that is upon it, he is guilty. Ye fools and blind: for whether *is* greater, the gift, or the altar that sanctifieth the gift? Whoso therefore shall swear by the altar, sweareth by it, and by all things thereon. And whoso shall swear by the temple, sweareth by it, and by him that dwelleth therein. And he that shall swear by heaven, sweareth by the throne of God, and by him that sitteth thereon. (vv. 16–22)

Everything in the world is inter-related, Jesus taught, and is hierarchically ranked—and ends in the throne room of God. Those logic-chopping casuists who justify this sin and condemn that virtue are dismissed for what they are—*fools and blind*. The man who swears on a leather-bound Bible has to keep his oath. The man who swears on a paperback is not obligated. Right. These guys were a real piece of work.

> Woe unto you, scribes and Pharisees, hypocrites! for ye pay tithe of mint and anise and cummin, and have omitted the weightier matters of the law, judgment, mercy, and faith: these ought ye to have done, and not to leave the other undone. Ye blind guides, which strain at a gnat, and swallow a camel. Woe unto you, scribes and Pharisees, hypocrites! for ye make clean the outside of the cup and of the platter, but within they are full of extortion and excess. Thou blind Pharisee, cleanse first that which is within the cup and platter, that the outside of them may be clean also. Woe unto you, scribes and Pharisees, hypocrites! for ye are like unto whited sepulchres, which indeed appear beautiful outward, but are within full of dead men's bones, and of all uncleanness. Even so ye also outwardly appear righteous unto men, but within ye are full of hypocrisy and iniquity. (vv. 23–28; Lk. 11:39)

They had two basic problems here. First, they had no sense of proportion. They would pay Judas money to betray the Messiah, but then when Judas returned the money, they had profound scruples about which account they put it in! We just paid this guy to betray Israel's hope and glory, and he brought the money back. What do we do now? We can't put the blood money back in the Temple coffers. That would be a *sin*. The second problem they had was the reason for the first. Because they only cared about appearances, and not about realities, as long as those appearances were kept up, nothing else mattered. They were decorated tombs, and as long as visitors stayed upwind, everything was fine. The incongruities can be very public, for a long time, just as long as everyone agrees to not notice. But when a prophet comes along and starts pointing things out, there is nowhere to hide. And this is why prophets die as often as they do.

The result of this kind of folly was that they had no sense of historical covenant awareness.

> Woe unto you, scribes and Pharisees, hypocrites! because ye build the tombs of the prophets, and garnish the sepulchres of the righteous, And say, If we had been in the days of our fathers, we would not have been partakers with them in the blood of the prophets. Wherefore ye be witnesses unto yourselves, that ye are the children of them which killed the prophets. Fill ye up then the measure of your fathers. Ye serpents, ye generation of vipers, how can ye escape the damnation of hell? (vv. 29–32)

American history is by no means sacred history, but it does provide us with very funny illustrations of this same mentality. Washington, D.C. is filled with monuments and statues to people whose civil convictions would get them lynched if they came back today by some time machine fluke to occupy public office. George Washington comes to mind. Not to mention Madison, Jefferson, and Adams.

As the Lord established earlier, the scribes and Pharisees were tombs themselves, and this is why they liked to decorate the tombs of righteous men. In doing this, they proved to Jesus that they were actually the children of those who had killed the prophets. Their concern for the prophets' tombs testified against them. In a similar way, modern evangelicals really like names such as Wycliff or Tyndale. Our forebearers! But one edifying thought experiment (there are many such) consists of William Tyndale paying a tumultuous visit to Tyndale House, publishers of the inane *Left Behind* series. One pictures broken windows, crying secretaries, sirens, a major scene, an arrest, and a board meeting the next day with the suits and haircuts trying to decide if they should press charges against this very troubled man. At the end they decide to just make him pay for the damage he did to the sign out front— the sign that had his name on it. This is an obvious point, but a certain kind of mind still misses it. This is because a certain kind of mind couldn't hit a bull on the ass with a banjo.

> Wherefore, behold, I send unto you prophets, and wise men, and scribes: and some of them ye shall kill and crucify; and some of them shall ye scourge in your synagogues, and persecute them from city to city: That upon you may come all the righteous blood shed upon the earth, from the blood of righteous Abel unto the blood of Zacharias son of Barachias, whom ye slew between the temple and the altar. Verily I say unto you, All these things shall come upon this generation. O Jerusalem, Jerusalem, thou that killest the prophets, and stonest them which are sent unto thee, how often would I have gathered thy children together, even as

a hen gathereth her chickens under her wings, and ye
would not! Behold, your house is left unto you desolate.
For I say unto you, Ye shall not see me henceforth, till
ye shall say, Blessed is he that cometh in the name of
the Lord. (vv. 34–39; cf. Mk. 7:9–13)

And this is why these things end in bloodshed. There is
no answer that can be given to the righteous prophet. Because
he is righteous, he is right. Because he is a prophet, he won't
shut up. He has fire in his bones. And so it is good that he
perish—of course, for the public good. He was a trouble-
maker anyway, and his language frequently went outside the
boundaries of respectable academic discourse.

But the story does not end there. Jesus rose from the dead
and ascended into heaven. From the right hand of God the
Father, He decreed the judgment that would fall upon Jerusalem in A.D. 70. And here is the final lesson of this chapter.
In the long run, stupidity doesn't work. Those who are fools
and blind cannot lead—except into a ditch.

In ages when folly reigns, the lot of a satirist is frequently
very difficult. For example, if I were to say that a church
somewhere had devoted the evening service to a display of
professional wrestling, in crazy times the reader would not
know if I were making this up or not. In the same way, we are
not sure if first-century almsgiving was really conducted with
literal fanfare and flourishes, with literal trumpets before-
hand. Was there a time when those giving alms felt comfortable in telling the whole world what they were doing, acting
like an eight-year-old standing on the high dive? "Everybody,
look at *meeeee!*"

Therefore when thou doest thine alms, do not sound a trumpet before thee, as the hypocrites do in the synagogues and in the streets, that they may have glory of men. Verily I say unto you, They have their reward. (Mt. 6:2)

But whether this was a literal description or not, the fact remains that Jesus tells us about it in a way that makes the ludicrous nature of it very clear.

Jesus even makes fun of how men *pray*. Jesus, the One in whose name we pray, during His incarnate ministry, leveled the guns of satire at those who sought to "have a witness" by praying openly in restaurants so that people could see how holy they were. Jesus told us not to pray so that men could see us, which we have interpreted as a call to hold public prayer vigils on the Capitol steps so that Congress will stop disobeying what Jesus said to do.

And when thou prayest, thou shalt not be as the hypocrites are: for they love to pray standing in the synagogues and in the corners of the streets, that they may be seen of men. Verily I say unto you, They have their reward. (Mt. 6:5)

Not only that, He thinks their fasting is funny too, particularly the part where they put on make-up so that others will see how gaunt and pale they are.

Moreover when ye fast, be not, as the hypocrites, of a sad countenance: for they disfigure their faces, that they may appear unto men to fast. Verily I say unto you, They have their reward. (Mt. 6:16)

When Jesus is teaching against anxiety and worry, He uses the striking image of those who run out of worries for the day, and so they have to get an advance. I don't have enough troubles—and so I have to borrow some from next week. "Take therefore no thought for the morrow: for the morrow shall take thought for the things of itself. Sufficient unto the day *is* the evil thereof" (Mt. 6:34).

He also took a dim view of those insufferable critics who are never satisfied. If a righteous man comes to them doing something, they wish he had come doing the opposite. But when the next righteous man comes along doing that very thing, lo and behold, now their preference goes back to the first guy.

> But whereunto shall I liken this generation? It is like unto children sitting in the markets, and calling unto their fellows, and saying, We have piped unto you, and ye have not danced; we have mourned unto you, and ye have not lamented. For John came neither eating nor drinking, and they say, He hath a devil. The Son of man came eating and drinking, and they say, Behold a man gluttonous, and a winebibber, a friend of publicans and sinners. But wisdom is justified of her children. (Mt. 11:16–19; Lk. 7:31–35)

Jesus was not above using ethnic humor to make His point either.

> And, behold, a woman of Canaan came out of the same coasts, and cried unto him, saying, Have mercy on me, O Lord, thou Son of David; my daughter is grievously

vexed with a devil. But he answered her not a word. And his disciples came and besought him, saying, Send her away; for she crieth after us. But he answered and said, I am not sent but unto the lost sheep of the house of Israel. Then came she and worshipped him, saying, Lord, help me. But he answered and said, It is not meet to take the children's bread, and to cast it to dogs. And she said, Truth, Lord: yet the dogs eat of the crumbs which fall from their masters' table. Then Jesus answered and said unto her, O woman, great is thy faith: be it unto thee even as thou wilt. And her daughter was made whole from that very hour. (Mt. 15:22–28; Mk. 7:27)

My understanding of this encounter is that Jesus was pulling his disciples' chain. This woman was not a Jew, and the Jews had problems dealing with such people, considering them beneath contempt—in a word, *dogs*. Put in terms that we might be more familiar with, Jesus was white, and the disciples were white, and this black woman comes up seeking healing for her daughter. She gets ignored. The disciples ask Jesus to send her off. She comes up and beseeches Christ for healing. It's not right, He says, to give perfectly good white folk food to "niggers." Disciples mentally cheer. But she sees the look in His eye, and the inverted commas around the epithet, and answers in kind. He relents, which was His intent all along, and heals the woman's daughter. If this understanding is right, then Jesus was using a racial insult to make a point. If it is not correct, then He was simply using a racial insult. In either case, His language is more than a little rough.

All things considered, we can see that Christ's use of satire in controversy hardly qualifies him as the original verbal pacifist. Quite the reverse. If there is anyone in Scripture who uses this form of expression as the most normal thing in the world, it is the Lord.

FOUR
Old Testament Satire and Jabs

We have noted that the Bible contains much satire. And while it is possible to overstate this point, our dangers generally lie in the other direction—the direction of assuming that we have biblical warrant for that which is sweety-nice. In other words, the real dilemma should confront those who would undertake a biblical defense of writing like the author of the Elsie Dinsmore stories. While there are things in the Bible that might even resemble Swift's *Modest Proposal*, there is nothing that remotely resembles nineteenth century sentimentality. So why is it that those who write such things never have to give a biblical defense of what they are doing? And why do I have to write this book defending a scriptural approach, and those who write books with titles like *When Throbs the Heart* never have to explain themselves at all? The answer is that such authors are writing for a modern evangelical audience, and "the trees of the Lord are full of sap" (Ps. 104:16).

Nevertheless, that's the way it is, and so we might as well just soldier through. The book of Amos is a satiric book, and the tone is frequently sarcastic and thoroughly Juvenalian.

Woe to them that are at ease in Zion, and trust in the mountain of Samaria, which are named chief of the nations, to whom the house of Israel came! Pass ye unto Calneh, and see; and from thence go ye to Hamath the great: then go down to Gath of the Philistines: be they better than these kingdoms? or their border greater than your border? Ye that put far away the evil day, and cause the seat of violence to come near; that lie upon beds of ivory, and stretch themselves upon their couches, and eat the lambs out of the flock, and the calves out of the midst of the stall; that chant to the sound of the viol, and invent to themselves instruments of music, like David; that drink wine in bowls, and anoint themselves with the chief ointments: but they are not grieved for the affliction of Joseph. (Amos 6:1–6)

Woe, in other words, to those who roll around on their beds like they were really something, with mirrors on the ceiling, pink champagne on ice. These people think they are rock stars at the Grammies, gathered together with *all* the glitterati, all ready to receive the award for Best Album, and with a prepared acceptance speech that will display to the whole world the fact that they have the emotional needs of a sucking chest wound. California did not invent these hollow people; the prophet Amos had them nailed centuries ago.

But this is not the only kind of sin that is lampooned in the Old Testament. The sluggard is a favorite target. "As the door turneth upon his hinges, so doth the slothful upon his bed" (Prov. 26:14). Just like the door to the kitchen in a busy restaurant turns, back and forth, back and forth, so the sluggard works industriously back and forth between the sheets. We have to get this into our minds—the Bible makes fun of sluggards *sinning*.

Then we have the ancient Hebrew equivalent of "aliens kidnapped me, what year is it?" The lazy man's excuses are a wonderful font of creativity. "The slothful man saith, There is a lion without, I shall be slain in the streets" (Prov. 22:13). Why aren't you out looking for a job? "Well, I was afraid that radiation from the traffic lights might give me cancer." "A slothful man hideth his hand in his bosom, and will not so much as bring it to his mouth again" (Prov. 19:24). That man is so lazy—how lazy is he? He is as lazy as a dog I had that needed to lean his head against the wall to bark.

The self-important busybody and meddler is always an important target for those who would be wise. "He that passeth by, and meddleth with strife belonging not to him, is like one that taketh a dog by the ears" (Prov. 26:17). And this meddlesome fellow is often an early riser. "He that blesseth his friend with a loud voice, rising early in the morning, it shall be counted a curse to him" (Prov. 27:14).

The Bible even goes in for a little bimbo humor. "As a jewel of gold in a swine's snout, so is a fair woman which is without discretion" (Prov. 11:22). Here, let us consider the parable. Is feminine beauty worth anything? Absolutely, between three and four hundred dollars an ounce. But what is her lack of discretion like? It is like six hundred pounds of porcine ugliness, fat, sassy, bristle-backed, and chewing on a root. But still the beauty is the central thing, and is given the place of honor, right there in the middle of our word picture, hanging on the snout. And the humor is that of a shrewd and homely peasant wisdom.

A nagging wife is like a leaking faucet, which is ironic, because that is probably what she was nagging him *about*—"the contentions of a wife are a continual dropping" (Prov. 19:13; cf. 27:15).

We find the same kind of images in Ecclesiastes.

He that diggeth a pit shall fall into it; and whoso breaketh an hedge, a serpent shall bite him. Whoso removeth stones shall be hurt therewith; and he that cleaveth wood shall be endangered thereby. If the iron be blunt, and he do not whet the edge, then must he put to more strength: but wisdom is profitable to direct. Surely the serpent will bite without enchantment; and a babbler is no better. . . . The labour of the foolish wearieth every one of them, because he knoweth not how to go to the city. (Eccl. 10:8–11, 15)

In other words, in our idiom, there was a fellow who went into the hardware store to complain about the chain saw he had purchased. The advertisement had claimed that he could cut four cords in an afternoon, and he had only been able to do one. The clerk didn't understand it and went out into the parking lot and pulled on the rope start, and the startled customer shied away. "What's that noise?" If you want to cut the wood, Solomon says, *sharpen the blade*.

And the fool who throws rocks at the moon shouldn't be surprised when they fall back down on his head. And there is another fool who works himself into a lather trying to hit the ground with his hat. He could get lost trying to stay on the sidewalk.

The book of Job contains some very pointed sarcasm, first from Job to his friends, and then from the Lord to Job. "And Job answered and said, No doubt but ye are the people, and wisdom shall die with you" (Job 12:1–2). And of course, when God appears at the end of the book, He demands that Job stand and deliver.

> Then the LORD answered Job out of the whirlwind, and said, Who *is* this that darkeneth counsel by words without knowledge? Gird up now thy loins like a man; for I will demand of thee, and answer thou me. Where wast thou when I laid the foundations of the earth? declare, if thou hast understanding. Who hath laid the measures thereof, if thou knowest? or who hath stretched the line upon it? (Job 38:1–5)

Who darkens counsel by giving counsel? Who obscures with words, when words were given to cast light? "Stand up, Job," God says. "Where were you when I created the universe? Where were you standing? What did you see? Tell me, since *you* know so much."

The message of the last chapters of the book is unrelenting. And the same basic point comes up again. Who is man to talk back to God? And if man *does* talk back to God, then perhaps it would be appropriate to refer to this sarcastically.

> Moreover the LORD answered Job, and said, Shall he that contendeth with the Almighty instruct him? he

that reproveth God, let him answer it. Then Job answered the LORD, and said, Behold, I am vile; what shall
I answer thee? I will lay mine hand upon my mouth.
Once have I spoken; but I will not answer: yea, twice;
but I will proceed no further. (Job 40:1–5)

He who reproves God, setting up shop to instruct God,
let *him* answer these questions. When God rebukes Job out
of the whirlwind, Job has the humility and sense to cover his
mouth with his hand, thoroughly abashed. But modern evangelicals chatter on. They have embraced the theology of the
foolish women Job mentioned at the beginning of the book,
and, judging by the posters in their Bible and bauble stores,
are resolved to maintain, against all evidence, that their God
is the God of pussy willows, baskets of kittens, and other
religious paraphernalia dangerous to diabetics.

Idolatrous folly is deadly serious. The Bible never pretends
that it is not. But neither do the writers of Scripture assume
that deadly folly cannot be mocked, sometimes mercilessly.
And to do this does not place the biblical spokesman as one
who is sitting in the seat of mockers. Returning to an earlier
point, everything depends on what is mocked and from where.
The Lord holds the rebellions of men in derision, but He does
so from heaven. This does not make the right hand of God
the Father a "seat of mockers." The seat of mockers is that
place where men try to mock the things of heaven. Mocking
a god made out of stone or wood is a different proposition
altogether.

And Elijah said unto the prophets of Baal, Choose you
one bullock for yourselves, and dress it first; for ye are

many; and call on the name of your gods, but put no
fire under. And they took the bullock which was given
them, and they dressed it, and called on the name of
Baal from morning even until noon, saying, O Baal,
hear us. But there was no voice, nor any that answered.
And they leaped upon the altar which was made. And
it came to pass at noon, that *Elijah mocked them*, and said,
Cry aloud: for he is a god; either he is talking, or he
is pursuing, or he is in a journey, or peradventure he
sleepeth, and must be awaked. And they cried aloud,
and cut themselves after their manner with knives and
lancets, till the blood gushed out upon them. And it
came to pass, when midday was past, and they proph-
esied until the time of the offering of the evening sacri-
fice, that there was neither voice, nor any to answer, nor
any that regarded. (I Kgs. 18:25–29, emphasis added)

The passage is plain—Elijah mocked them. And in the
original Hebrew he is even more pointed. Perhaps your god
is off in the bathroom. His prophets are all gathered in the
hallway with an anxious look on their faces. Bang on the door
louder. He's been in there a long time.

Not only do we have Elijah's Juvenalian treatment of the
false prophets (which in itself was mild compared to what he
did to them *later* in the day), we also have the deft satire of the
writer of the narrative. The behavior of the false prophets was
extreme, to say the least, and the writer says, tongue in cheek,
"But there was no voice, nor any that answered." In an exqui-
site juxtaposition, the writer tells us about the frenzy of the
idolaters—loud yells, self-mutilation, blood gushing—and

then says again, "there was neither voice, nor any to answer, nor any that regarded."

After Elijah's taunts about how Baal was off in the bathroom, sitting on his throne, we might want to reconsider our glib assumption that there is never a godly place for scatological humor. And this brings us to the mocking narrative about Ehud, a left-handed deliverer of Israel, and Eglon, the obese tyrant. The story is what is called a slave narrative, with an oppressed people having fun at the expense of the established powers that be.

But before proceeding further with this illustration, I have to tell one of our own family's stories, one that has made Eglon's demise part of our own set of treasured memories. One time when my oldest daughter, Bekah, was a very young girl, she was having a hard time of it and was out of sorts. It was not the kind of thing that merited overt discipline, and so my wife suggested that Bekah go off to her bedroom and read in her Bible for a little bit. After a short time, a small voice came out of the bedroom—"Mom, where is that place where the fat king got stabbed and the fat covered over the sword?" Nothing like a happy story to cheer you up on a rainy day.

The people of Israel cried out to God, and He gave them a left-handed deliverer from the tribe of Benjamin. Israel used Ehud to send tribute, and there is a quaint double meaning here—"Israel sent a present unto Eglon" (Judg. 3:15). Ehud made a two-edged dagger, and, being left-handed, strapped it to his right thigh, under his clothing (v. 16). The security screeners of Moab were federal workers, asleep at their stations, and so Ehud got in. The tribute was delivered, and we discover that Eglon was a "very fat man" (v. 17). Ehud delivered the goods, and then he dismissed everyone who had come with him bearing the tribute, a move calculated to make the Moabites relax their guard even further (v. 18). He told Eglon that he had a secret message, and so Eglon dismissed everyone (vv. 19–20). Ehud came to him in his own private pavilion and told the king that he had a message to him from God (v. 20). Eglon stood up and Ehud said, "God loves you and has a wonderful plan for your life, what's left of it." At that point, Ehud took his dagger and ran it into the king. The fat closed over it, and Ehud lost a perfectly good dagger. The contents of Eglon's intestines came out, giving Ehud an additional reason to leave—which he did, locking the doors behind him (v. 23). The Moabite servants came to the pavilion doors, and, finding them locked, assumed from the smell that Eglon was taking care of business (v. 24). They hung out until the whole thing got embarrassing, then got a key, opened the doors, and lo! Their lord was "fallen down dead on the earth" (v. 25). In the meantime, Ehud had a good head start, rallied the troops, and organized, to use our terminology, a successful anti-government protest (vv. 26–30).

Nothing is more serious than the sin of idolatry, but this did not keep the prophets from making fun of it. The first thing Isaiah notes is how *hard* certain men have to work when they are making their god. Hard work being a deity-smith.

> The smith with the tongs both worketh in the coals, and fashioneth it with hammers, and worketh it with the strength of his arms: yea, he is hungry, and his strength faileth: he drinketh no water, and is faint. (Is. 44:12)

Not only is the fashioning of deity hard physical labor, it takes a good deal of shrewd discernment. It is not just anybody who can look at a log and see which end of it should be used for cooking dinner and which end should become the object of worship and adoration.

> Then shall it be for a man to burn: for he will take thereof, and warm himself; yea, he kindleth it, and baketh bread; yea, he maketh a god, and worshippeth it; he maketh it a graven image, and falleth down thereto. (v. 15)

Not one to let a good jibe go, Isaiah develops the point.

> He burneth part thereof in the fire; with part thereof he eateth flesh; he roasteth roast, and is satisfied: yea, he warmeth himself, and saith, Aha, I am warm, I have seen the fire: And the residue thereof he maketh a god, even his graven image: he falleth down unto it, and worshippeth it, and prayeth unto it, and saith, Deliver me; for thou art my god. (vv. 16–17)

As all wise woodworkers knew, the part for making one's own savior is the "residue." This monstrosity is an example of extreme spiritual blindness. "They have not known nor understood: for he hath shut their eyes, that they cannot see; *and* their hearts, that they cannot understand" (v. 18). But the fact that we are dealing with lost heathen is not taken by God's prophet as reason for laying off. These are people who have deceived hearts, and they have a lie in their right hand (v. 20). Regardless, Isaiah answers a fool according to his folly, lest he puff himself up and become wise in his own eyes.

Abigail was an intelligent and beautiful woman, and an insightful judge of character when it came to her own husband, who was named Nabal. The Hebrew form of his name might be rendered loosely as "blockhead," which comes out when Abigail is busy saving his life as she intercedes with David. Incidentally, *Belial* here means *worthlessness.*

> Let not my lord, I pray thee, regard this man of Belial, even Nabal: for as his name is, so is he; Nabal is his name, and folly is with him: but I thine handmaid saw not the young men of my lord, whom thou didst send. (I Sam. 25:25)

David himself was capable of letting loose, and on one occasion he really unloaded a first-class curse. Joab, an influential commander under David, had taken the opportunity for revenge provided by Abner when he abandoned his king, Ishbosheth. Earlier Abner had killed Joab's brother in battle, and Joab took the peace provided by the negotiations as the right time for killing Abner. This he did, and David did not have enough political power to punish or remove Joab—as much as he wanted to. But David could distance himself from Joab's action, and he did so by means of a curse that, if we think about it, singes the eyebrows.

> Let it rest on the head of Joab, and on all his father's house; and let there not fail from the house of Joab one that hath an issue, or that is a leper, or that leaneth on a staff, or that falleth on the sword, or that lacketh bread. (2 Sam. 3:29)

This is not to say that Old Testament writers were incapable of ironic understatement. I have sometimes thought about writing an article advocating the courtship model found in the book of Ruth—work hard in the field at harvest, have enough to drink to make the heart merry and sleep sweet, go to sleep on the threshing floor, and wake up in the middle of the night to find a beautiful woman sleeping with you. The ironies of the situation were not lost on the first person to recount the story. And lo, it was a girl.

> And it came to pass at midnight, that the man was afraid, and turned himself: and, behold, a woman lay at his feet. And he said, Who art thou? And she answered, I am Ruth thine handmaid: spread therefore thy skirt over thine handmaid; for thou art a near kinsman. (Ruth 3:8–9)

Another instance of "lo, it was a girl" has to be considered one of the funniest and most tragic verses in the Bible. Jacob (already in his seventies) had worked for seven years to receive the hand of Rachel in marriage. The day of the wedding had finally come, but Laban pulled a switcheroo—indicating that wedding receptions can be dimly lit to the detriment of the groom. Or perhaps it means some of their wedding night customs differed from ours.

> And it came to pass, that in the morning, behold, it was Leah: and he said to Laban, What is this thou hast done unto me? did not I serve with thee for Rachel? wherefore then hast thou beguiled me? (Gen. 29:25)

Notice the quiet understatement here on the part of the bemused historian.

All these examples from the Old Testament serve to show us that verbal jabs are not necessarily a sin, and neither are verbal pummelings. Of course it is *possible* to sin by means of sarcasm and mocking, but how are we to tell the difference? The psalmist takes a dim view of mockers and scoffers as a class (Ps. 1). We know this in part because mockers are mocked—and this is no contradiction. The ultimate answer is that we are to be steeped in the language and practice of *all* of Scripture. Many of the pietistic objections to the serrated edge of biblical satire are simply the result of a highly selective reading.

The Bible tells us that wisdom does not come in a can. One size does not fit all. We are told not to answer a fool according to his folly because we run a risk of becoming like him (Prov. 26:4). We are told in the next breath to answer him according to his folly before he starts thinking he has won the debate (Prov. 26:5). When is which?

Before we can answer this question rightly, we have to *ask* it rightly. This is one of those situations where even to ask the question—"How do we tell the right time for satire and the right time for tenderness?"—answers those who want to say that there is never a time for polemical speech. But of course, as we have seen, this is just another example of something that pietists excel at doing—trying to be wiser than God, holier than God, *nicer* than God.

They have made an idol out of their own emotional predilections, and like the idolater whom Isaiah made fun of, they have a hard time telling which end of the log should cook dinner and which end of it should undergo an apotheosis. Which emotion should make me have a good cry and which one should be fashioned into the standard of all righteousness?

FIVE

The Language of Paul

Along with many other passages of Scripture, the apostle Paul teaches us the necessity of guarding our speech.

> Let all bitterness, and wrath, and anger, and clamour, and evil speaking, be put away from you, with all malice; and be ye kind one to another, tenderhearted, forgiving one another, even as God for Christ's sake hath forgiven you. (Eph. 4:31–32)

Some of the immediate applications that crowd into our minds are convicting to us personally, and they should continue to crowd us until we admit the righteousness of God's standards for our speech. This involves repentance—confessing sin to God (I Jn. 1:9)—and taking care to make any verbal restitution that is necessary because of our verbal sin. For example, children would confess bitterness to parents, parents would confess fits of anger to children, neighbors who have quarreled would acknowledge their "evil speaking." All this would be done in kindness, tender-heartedness, and be covered over with a spirit of forgiveness. And of course, we know that such a work is a gift from the Spirit of God. Whenever men live like this, the grace of God is evident.

But assume for a moment that a certain man has Paul's understanding of these words, and that he is obedient. He practices this standard—he is a kind man, biblically defined. But what are the *practical* boundaries that set the pattern for his verbal behavior? Can he write a sharp letter to the editor? Can he use sarcasm in a debate on the floor of presbytery? And does it matter what issue is being debated there? Ordination of women? When the presbytery will reconvene after lunch?

Our problem comes when we hear Paul's words and rush off to define them in accordance with the dictates of universal niceness. Then, if anyone engages in verbal polemics, he is promptly rebuked—"be ye *kind* one to another." But we must do here what we do with every other thorny problem of interpretation—define what Paul means in this place by looking at how he uses language throughout the rest of his epistles. Also we should look very carefully at what he actually says here; we are to be kind to *one another*. Sheep are to be kind to sheep. Shepherds are to be kind to sheep. But if a shepherd is kind to wolves, that is just another way to let them savage the sheep. Kindness to sheep is hostility to wolves. Kindness to wolves is hostility to sheep. All attempts to get the wolves and sheep together for some kind of an ecumenical lovefest will only result in fat, contented wolves.

We see this principle assumed when the apostle Paul confronts the Judaizers who were troubling the churches of Galatia.

And I, brethren, if I yet preach circumcision, why do I yet suffer persecution? then is the offence of the cross ceased. I would they were even cut off which trouble you. (Gal. 5:11–12)

This is a really loaded insult. First, Paul wishes that the false teachers, so zealous for cutting off the foreskins of certain Gentile others, would turn their attentions to their own Jewish selves, in order to cut the whole thing off. Second, this form of self-mutilation was common among pagans and shows that Paul has a real contempt for the tenets of the circumcision party—in his mind, it is no better than Baal worship. And last, the language "cut off" makes us think of more than just the missing *membrum virile*. Someone mutilated in the way desired by Paul was excluded from the Temple worship of the old covenant—he was cut off from the covenant people. Every way you look at it, these super Jews were not Jews at all. It should be obvious that Paul is handling his opponents somewhat roughly. And, in order to reinforce the point of this entire section, his behavior should help us define what *he* means when he says that our speech should be gracious, seasoned with *salt* (Col. 4:6).

The truly astonishing thing for many modern readers (were we to notice) is how Paul continues. Right after he says that he wishes his theological opponents would overachieve and cut off more than they were currently advocating, he then goes on, in the next breath, to urge the Galatians to a life of love. The Galatians had been called to liberty but should not use that liberty as an occasion for serving themselves. Rather, they should by love serve one another (Gal. 5:13). In plain language, Paul is urging the self-castration of his adversaries in verse 12 and is urging an ethic of love in verse 13. And he goes on. The whole law is summed up in the second greatest commandment, which is to love our neighbors as we love ourselves (v. 14). He then warns the Galatians against biting and devouring one another, lest they consume one another (v. 15). All of this immediately follows his avowed desire that the world's population of eunuchs might rise. Clearly, if we accept the inspiration of Scripture, the love he is urging in verses 13–15 is not what our modern sentimentalist age believes that it is.

This was a subject about which Paul felt strongly, and there was a correspondence between how he felt and the way he expressed it. Dealing with the same subject in another epistle—the subject being self-righteous and smug religion—he says that he does not mind repeating himself (Phil. 3:1). Then he says, "Beware of dogs, beware of evil workers, beware of the concision" (3:2). Paul goes on to show that if there were anything to brag about here, then *he* would be able to brag about it. At one time, he was the ideal of the Jewish man (vv. 4–7). And he deliberately sets this model of religiosity up big and large so that he might have a good sized target.

> Yea doubtless, and I count all things but loss for the excellency of the knowledge of Christ Jesus my Lord: for whom I have suffered the loss of all things, and do count them but dung, that I may win Christ. (Phil. 3:8)

The King James is better than most, translating one particular word here as *dung*. The word is *skubalon*, and means in the first place some kind of animal excrement. And this verse helps show the problem we are in—Paul does teach elsewhere that we are to avoid filthiness in our speech, coarse jesting, and so on (Eph. 5:4). But we have taken this and over-refined it, absolutizing it in terms of latent-Victorian sensibilities. As a result we simply cannot imagine the lofty sentiment of this wonderful passage (e.g., the "excellency of the knowledge of Christ Jesus my Lord") functioning in the same sentence with *dog shit*. But there it is—Paul has scraped all self-important, prim and proper, fussy-tidy religion off the bottom of his shoe. Why? That he might win Christ.

Part of the reason why we might have trouble with this kind of forcefulness in language is that we do not have the same zeal to "win Christ." Of course, there are boys in junior high school who delight in bathroom humor, and they need to memorize Ephesians 5:4—so that *they* might win Christ. No one is maintaining that Christians should routinely speak or write in some foul fashion. Paul prohibits it.

But when certain key issues are at stake, and the verbal equivalent of a tactical nuclear strike is needed from the preacher, the Scriptures show us in a number of places that the prophetic preacher comes through. Ezekiel uses calculated moral obscenities, designed to shake up the complacent (Ezek. 23:19–21). Isaiah, attacking the same attitude of religiosity that Paul hated so much, compares all our attempts at self-justification to nothing more than a used menstrual cloth (Is. 64:6). And Paul speaks as noted above.

And depend upon it—modern evangelicals will be far more upset with my *use* of a certain phrase in the passage above than they are by the fact that many of our popular religious practices, customs, and superstitions *smell* like that phrase. They feel this way because their scriptural categories are inverted. Fools and blind! Why does the living room stink? Is it the shoe or what you tracked in with the shoe?

Far more is involved in learning how to do this than just making a list of words that can be used—whether never, occasionally, or all the time. Someone who has a generally pietistic cast of mind cannot just throw a word in here or there—that would be like trying to play honky tonk music on the piccolo. All of our language needs to be shaped by Scripture, and this includes vocabulary, motives, demeanor, content, balance, and so on. And one of the basic points of this small book is that the Bible is not the kind of book that many Christians have glibly assumed it to be.

In his polemical warfare, Paul does not hesitate to go after certain people by name.

> This charge I commit unto thee, son Timothy, according to the prophecies which went before on thee, that thou by them mightest war a good warfare; Holding faith, and a good conscience; which some having put away concerning faith have made shipwreck: Of whom is Hymenaeus and Alexander; whom I have delivered unto Satan, that they may learn not to blaspheme. (I Tim. 1:18–20)

And again, in another place, he notes:

> Alexander the coppersmith did me much evil: the Lord reward him according to his works: Of whom be thou ware also; for he hath greatly withstood our words. (2 Tim. 4:14)

This is as good a place as any to make note of the fact that public controversy is not bound by the rules of confrontation laid out for us in Matthew 18. When Peter sinned at Antioch, Paul rebuked him publicly, face to face (Gal. 2:11), and he did this on the spot. It is not necessary to take someone aside privately after they have just done something publicly. I do not know how many times I have been asked about this. Let's say I have written critically of a recently published book— "Did you contact Tony Campolo privately before you wrote the book review?"

The conclusion of the matter is that Paul, like so many other biblical writers, uses hard, satiric language. He differs from the Lord Jesus in that the Lord's jibes were frequently very "laugh out loud" funny. Paul's satire is much more business-like and serious, but this is simply a function of his personality. He was an apostle who liked to stay on task. I have no doubt that Paul had a highly developed sense of humor (as a dinner companion), but this does not really come out in the book of Ephesians. But in any case, whether serious or humorous, we see yet again the ongoing utility of having a scriptural satiric bite.

SIX

Dearlybelovedism

In some ways, gross sin is simple—it is easy to identify. Everyone knows that it is not right to run a scam on your grandmother in order to bilk her out of her life savings. Depending on a person's disposition and personality, some of these overt sins will be alluring and some will not be. But all of them are alluring to *somebody*. A sin that was never attractive to anyone would not make it into our lexicon of sinning. No one would do it, and we wouldn't have a name for it.

For Christians, the difficulty with such overt sins is not in understanding that repentance is required. Everyone who struggles with lust, or with a bad temper, or greed, knows that the sin is wrong—even though it is attractive anyway. And too often we think that our struggle with sanctification is a simple matter of overcoming the temptations to all these big E on the eye chart kinds of sins.

But it is not quite so simple. The real problem for many devout Christians, the hidden reef where many pietists have shipwrecked, is the problem posed by what we *think* are our virtues. And correspondingly, this is where a satirist can start to get into real trouble. If a satirist were to go after a minister who was a well-known lecherous drunk, there would be many among the pietists who would not mount such an attack themselves, but would not be all that bothered by it. But if an attack is mounted on someone who is generally respected, and if the target is respected because he is, taking one thing with another, a smarmy collection of gooey and correct sentiments, then defenders of that person can get really irate. It is one thing to attack murder, rape and pillage. It is quite another to attack prayers, rosaries, inspirational study Bibles, John 3:16 skateboards, and counseling pastors who exude empathy for a fee. These attacks run the risk of being mistaken for an attack on that which is actually being defended. If I saw someone approaching a priceless Vermeer painting with a can of orange spray paint, I would wrestle him to the ground—not as an enemy of art but as a friend of it. But in an insulated community of performance artists, the critic of art vandalism is likely to be thought of as an enemy of art itself.

The critic of Thomas Kinkade paintings, where all the puddles on the ground have this eerie radioactive glow, and all the bungalows look like the living room has just caught on fire, is assumed to be a critic who is hostile to home, hearth, and wholesome family values. But the actual object of his hostility is the misrepresentation of home and hearth—why must a friend of traditional values believe that the windows of homey little cottages must glow like they housed Nebuchadnezzar's furnace?

In the same way, the critic of Jesus junk stores is assumed to be a critic of Jesus. But of course, scriptural satire assumes that the foremost critic of Jesus junk stores would be Jesus Himself. If Christ were to go to the Christian Booksellers Association (CBA) convention and see all the crap being hawked with His name on it, He could spend all day there turning over the tables. The reason we have a problem with this, and not with the account of Christ cleansing the temple two thousand years ago, is that in this scenario, Christ is messing with *our* tables, *our* profits, *our* religious scams. Everybody is against two thousand year old sins. But it takes a prophet to be against the currently approved abominations.

So one of the central points of biblical satire is that we must not only repent of our sins, but also of those "virtues" for which we preen ourselves. We have trouble seeing such virtues as sinful, because we have neglected the essential practice of bringing the Word of God to bear on ourselves—not just ourselves back "when we were pagans," but ourselves currently as we make those lengthy prayers in the synagogues.

Our point of stumbling with regard to our religious "virtues" is warned against in 2 Corinthians 10:12. Those who compare themselves with themselves *are not wise.* Whenever a critic comes from the outside, he can see and point out the weirdness factor because he is not a participant in it. But whenever any claim to devotion or piety is accepted at face value within a given community of people, and cannot be challenged because it is Corban, devoted to God, the possible temptations associated with it become rapidly invisible to us. The people in this insular community—which is what the modern evangelical subcultural ghetto actually is—cannot see themselves.

Anyone who *can* see them, and talks about what they are doing, is *ipso facto* guilty of "arrogance." Having written these words, I realize that the phrase "evangelical subculture" can be taken two ways. And so I guess I mean it both ways.

And so this is how crass commercialism hides behind the veneer of evangelism. We have T-shirts with Christ the King designed to look like Calvin Klein. We have Tommy Hell-fighter stuff. We have gospel Frisbees. We have Testamints. We have Satan Stomper socks. Oppose any of this, and you are clearly deficient in evangelistic zeal. Don't you want the message to get *out*? Don't you want to see the lost won for Christ? The late Joseph Bayly wrote a delightful little book some years ago called *The Gospel Blimp*, which lampooned the earlier forms of this kind of evangelistic absurdity, back when inane evangelicalism was still slogging it out in the minors. It is hard to imagine what a man of his gifts would do with the embarrassment of riches he would face if he were here— trite evangelicalism has now had a long, sustained career in the majors and is now in the hall of fame. Born-againers are everywhere, and in virtually everything they touch they seek to make the holy things of the living God into a laughingstock. The faith that produced Augustine and Ambrose, Chrysostom and Calvin, Hodge and Edwards, is now busy trying to evangelize the world by acting dumber than a bag of hammers.

This is how trite and superficial worship is passed off as though it were the joy of the Lord. The Bible tells us that we are to work out our salvation with fear and trembling. The Scriptures tell us that we are to worship God with reverence and godly fear, because our God is a consuming fire. But we have picked up a notion somewhere that worship ought to be breezy, flippant, casual, and above all, *fun*. My wife and I were recently on vacation, and being strangers in a strange land, we sought out a place to worship while there. We picked a place that, judging by the name, seemed safe enough. But the service started out with a thumping worship band playing some up-beat pep rally songs. One of these songs had something to do with God's love being "all around, all around." You would think I could remember *all* the words to it because they sang them about as many times as the Beatles sang that nah-nah-nah part in "Hey, Jude."

But this was not enough. One of the song leaders taught everybody how to imitate a lawn sprinkler, spinning in place, one arm straight out and the other hand behind the head. So here we were, sitting in the back row of a strange church, watching a room full of adults spinning around as though they were lawn sprinklers. One of the song leaders, flushed with enthusiasm, cried out, "Who says church isn't fun!" These dear misguided people thought they were honoring God through what they were doing, even though what they were actually doing was teetering on the edge of blasphemy. What does a biblical Christian do when confronted with something like this? The scriptural answer is plain—make fun of it.

But this kind of modern exuberance is a reaction to an older form of the same problem. Back before the liturgical monkey-shines began, American Christians preferred a quieter, more sentimental approach, but just as unbiblical—"I come, after all, to the garden alone, while the dew is still on the roses." Victorian schmaltz came out in the music, in literature, in manners, and in the sermons. The sermons were a mixture of high-brow pretentiousness and a strange nasal vocalization that I have called *holyspeak*. Ministers would walk up to the pulpit, taking care to hover two inches above the carpet, and—it is hard to reproduce this in print—would say something like, "Now, BRETTHHruhn LET USSSsss pray." The great Spurgeon, who lived during the golden age of this kind of thing, had no use for what he called "foppery in a minister" and the "aping of gentility." As he put it, "Molasses and other sugary matters are sickening to me. Jack-dandy in the pulpit makes me feel as Jehu did when he saw Jezebel's decorated head and painted face, and cried in indignation, 'Fling her down.'" [1]

We are to act biblically, and never to react. Reactions are not the same thing as reformations. The modern worship service was a reaction to the older sentimentalist treacle, and *initially* it provided a refreshing relief. I grew up in a church where I recall the glorious hymn "Holy, Holy, Holy" being sung as though it were a ball and chain, and as a boy I hated that song. I can still recall the excitement of the first *Christian* songs accompanied by a guitar. But this was reaction, not reformation, and, not surprisingly, we discover that our much more superficial music takes a lot less time to get old. "Holy, Holy, Holy" took many generations before it got old. "Shine, Jesus, Shine" takes about a half an hour to get there.

But in the same way, simple reaction *back* is not reformation either. Some die-hard traditionalist defenders of orthodusty have no more understanding of what *they* are doing than do the contemporary worship dervishes. And this is why we need the simple honesty of satire. Pietism is an inadequate protector

---

1. Charles Spurgeon, *Lectures to My Students* (Grand Rapids: Zondervan, 1954), 300–302.

of piety, which is why pietism invariably leads to impiety. A biblical and satiric eye will see and reject all affectation, regardless of what age contained it. The Scriptures teach us that an honest answer is like a kiss on the lips.

So whenever we are putting on pious airs, standing on a *faux* dignity, sitting with an air of pseudo-approachability, puffing ourselves up in the name of contemporary relevance or venerable traditions, we are doing nothing more than pumping balloon juice into overextended latex. And satire is the needle for just such occasions, the gift of merciful God.

SEVEN
ModEvism

A common question concerns the propriety of attacking fellow Christians. If satire is employed on secular humanists, evolutionists, radical lesbians, and so on, then go to it. Far fewer Christians have a problem with this. But when the sixteen inch guns are turned on fellow believers, a lot of concerns arise.

For example, suppose some satiric comments are made about a modern evangelical worship service during which the youth group presents a skit in which the youth pastor rides a unicycle; the "worship portion" of the service is of the "three chords, four songs, two hours" variety; the sermon, such as it was, was taken right off the internet; and so on. Taking one thing with another, this presents an inviting target. At the same time, these people generally vote pro-life, they are concerned about the general deterioration of our culture, their families are intact, and so forth. Why attack *these* people?

In the first place, the scenario is a good example of how we tend to kid ourselves. We do not really have data that shows that there is an appreciable difference between modern evangelical Americans and their secularist counterparts. They get divorced at about the same rate, their kids start getting into pornography, fornication and drugs around the same time, their businesses run on the same semi-dishonest business practices. At the time of the Reformation, one proverbial phrase in France was "as honest as a Huguenot." The hard working and conscientious French Calvinists found that their honesty became a byword among the unbelievers. Does anyone seriously believe that unbelieving Americans are about to coin a similar phrase any time soon? "As honest as an evangelical." It would fit on a bumper sticker, but it doesn't have the same self-justifying ring of "Christians aren't perfect, just forgiven." A few years ago, when my wife and I were building our house, we subcontracted out work for a number of various things to a number of vendors. We were only ripped off twice, and both times by professing evangelicals. The unbelievers delivered, but not the Christians. The assumption that there is a drastic difference between nonbelievers and modern evangelicals appears to be a case of self-flattery. We have believed our own propaganda, which is not the same thing as believing the Bible.

But in the second place, let us assume for a moment that there is an appreciable difference of this practical kind between modern evangelicals and their secularist counterparts. We should take careful note of what is happening here. If we say that our lunacy on the Lord's Day ought not to be held up for public ridicule, then we are actually justifying disrespect of God's holy name, so long as certain horizontal "pieties" are maintained with regard to other human beings. Put bluntly, disrespect of God is all right as long as you don't want the kind of Supreme Court justices that the Democratic candidate would appoint. If that is not a good working summary of humanism, I do not know what is.

Related to this, we have to remember that ideas have consequences, as Richard Weaver taught us. Ideas take us places, and frequently we find ourselves in places where we had no conscious intention of going. The liberals of the 1920's did not anticipate the bizarre harvest we can now see in the mainstream denominations. If they had been warned about it, their only response would have been a confident laugh. The foolish alarmist who warned them of the eventual arrival of lesbian choir directors and Buddhist Presbyterian pastors would have been dismissed as a nutcase. But, right on schedule, here we are.

In the same way, modern evangelicals do not see that apart from a true worship of God, the "horizontal pieties" are not long for this world. Their current emphasis on family and social responsibilities at the expense of honoring God in appropriate worship is doomed to failure. Of course, emphasis on cultural engagement and family reformation is wonderful in its rightful place, which is when it is subordinated to the reverent worship of God—through Word and sacrament. Any other emphasis is simply refried liberalism in the great taco of unbelief. So even if it is *not* currently true that there is no distinction between the evangelical movement and the world, the lessons of Church history show us that in the very near future, it *will* be true.

So then, why is modern evangelicalism a legitimate target of biblical satire? Given the fact that we sin in so many creative ways, the answer can ultimately be as many-faceted as our own capacity for rationalization. But at the same time, there are some basic principles.

First, modern evangelicalism is a legitimate target because to whom much is given, much is required. It would be easy to assume that our attacks on modern evangelicalism are the result of some kind of contempt for the heritage of evangelicalism. But actually the reverse is the case. We are hard on modern evangelicalism because *it* has contempt for its own heritage. We have a high level of respect for what this movement *used* to be.

Scripture tells us that folly in a wise man stands out more than folly in a fool (Eccl. 10:1). A clean white shirt, well-ironed and starched, will reveal the great blob of catsup far more effectively than an old grungy shirt will. And this is why I am indignant that the heirs of Charles Hodge and R. L. Dabney and Jonathan Edwards, to speak only of Americans, are named Bill Bright, Bill Hybels, and Tony Campolo.

In the second place, modern evangelicalism is a legitimate target because judgment begins with the household of God (1 Pet. 4:17). We have a tendency to assume the opposite. *We* are the people of God, so the thinking goes, and so therefore when God starts His work of chastising and judging, He will not really have to deal with us "not-perfect-just-forgiven" types. But this misses God's pattern of work in the world. He deals with His people first, and in dealing with them sets an example for the world.

So before there can be any kind of restoration of national dignity in the civil realm, there must absolutely be a reformation in the Church—top to bottom, stem to stern, from the

front of the face to the back of the head. Modern evangelicalism is not the solution to America's problems, modern evangelicalism *is* America's problem. None of our general cultural
malaise will be mitigated in the least degree unless and until
a thorough work of God sweeps through the Church.

Many evangelicals think they acknowledge this, and they
call what they yearn for revival. But as A. W. Tozer put it, if
revival means more of what we have now, we most emphati-
cally do not need a revival. A reformation is necessary—a reformation that is in the first place liturgical, in the second place
familial, in the third place doctrinal, and in the fourth place,
cultural. We need to be shaken badly so that what cannot be
shaken may remain. In this reformation, we will—with tears
of repentance—throw away the vast machinery of parachurch
organizations, our glossy magazines edited by snakes, our en-
gineered revivalism, our holy hucksterism, our trivialization of
the gospel through dumb tracts, our attempts to save America
through politics, our corrupt youth ministries, and our gold-
painted thrones on TBN. There are more things that could
be mentioned, but a repentant mind can get the drift. In an
evangelical world filled to the brim with such things, it is astonishing that some people think that *satire* is a problem and
might invoke the displeasure of God.

Third, modern evangelicalism is a legitimate target because
the religious sins that are characteristic of modern evangelicals correspond readily to those sins that are attacked by the
biblical writers. As we ask ourselves how to imitate the pattern
set for us by Scripture, we have to note the correspondence
between that day and ours. The favored target of biblical writers is religious pomposity, of which modern evangelicals have

many surplus tons, stored in giant warehouses, piled up in heaps and mounds. Our sins are comparable to the ancient sins, our defensiveness is comparable, our shiftiness is comparable, and our hard-heartedness in the name of God is comparable. They appealed to the God of Abraham while seeking to kill Abraham's lord and master, while modern evangelicals emphasize a personal relationship with a sibilant Jeeeesussss while scorning His word, Spirit, and Church.

In the fourth place, modern evangelicalism is a legitimate target because of the claim to be a "people of the Book." We are Bible people, and we name our churches Bible churches, and we go to Bible studies, although Bibles are increasingly rare at them, and our holy hardware stores make megabucks selling study Bibles for "whatever ails ya." But the problem with making up titles of such Bible versions to illustrate a point here is that no matter how absurd I get, there is no doubt someone out there doing something comparable "for real." These are difficult days to be a satirist. But I will do my best anyhow. And so we have study Bibles for owners of King Charles cocker spaniels, study Bibles for litigious OPC pastors, study Bibles for the skateboarding youth of today, and study Bibles for Third Wives of Promise Keepers.

Helpfully supplementing all the study Bibles—published for a people who would not know what *study* was if it poked them in the eye with a burnt stick—are a vast plethora of translations. At the top of the list is the new publication put out by the International Bible Society, in cahoots with Zondervan, which is owned by Rupert Murdoch, who publishes soft porn in his *Sun* newspaper in the UK. This exciting new translation is designed to get fifteen-year-old boys back in the Word. Called the P3IV, the maps and concordance in the back have been replaced by glossy photos of topless women, taken from the *Sun's* page 3. Hence we have the clever moniker for the Bible of teenaged mouth-breathers. It has to be said that this move is controversial in some conservative circles. It also has to be said that I made up the second part—but not the first part. The publisher of the NIV *is* a soft pornographer, but we would draw the line if Larry Flynt of *Hustler* magazine were to try this. Wouldn't we?

Of course if we were to *open* these endless new translations of the Bible and read what they actually have to say, and note what the biblical writers make fun of, it is difficult to avoid the conclusion that someone ought to engage in a little incarnational application, starting with the publisher. I am reminded of the time I was reading Augustine's wonderful work *The City of God*, and I came to the part where he was making fun of the pagan priests for wearing their silly mitres for hats. I thought to myself, *huh*, I thought, and flipped the book over for another look at the cover. There was the bishop of Hippo, helpfully and artistically rendered by some pious soul who thought Augustine would look good in a mitre.

And so the word that should come to modern evangelicals who do not like being on the business end of a sharp, pointy object is a simple one. "*You* have given us permission to do this. How? you may ask. Well, we read about how Isaiah spoke to the compromisers of his day, and we read all about it in your *Study Bible for Menopausal Skateboarders*. If you want us to stop, then you need to stop selling those things."

This relates to the fifth point, which is that modern evangelicalism is a legitimate target because the things that modern evangelicals do are just so darn funny. This does not need to be developed at length. The reader is encouraged to simply ask to receive a Christian Book Distributor catalog, or tune in to the Trinity Broadcasting Network, for hours of innocent merriment and fun.

And last, with a faint note of optimism, modern evangelicalism is a legitimate target because the evangelical church is the most likely to profit from such attacks. Although Jesus did His best to make the party name Pharisee into a term of derision, and although it has to be said that He succeeded, the Scriptures clearly show that there were many godly Pharisees. Quite a number of them came to the faith, and one of them wrote the majority of the New Testament. In the same way, I know that in the world of the modern evangelical there are seven thousand who have not bowed the knee to Baal. But how can they be identified? They are the ones who acknowledge the *justice* of these charges, despite the extreme satire that is necessary given the evangelical insolence. Modern evangelicals who are the problem say, "But . . . ." Godly evangelicals will say, "That hurts. God have mercy."

EIGHT

Spurgeon the Magnificent

While in the course of preparing this book, I had the joy of coming across a small (and very entertaining) book by Charles Spurgeon called *Eccentric Preachers*.[1] While he was addressing preaching, not writing, it was remarkable how many of the same issues are involved. For the most part, Spurgeon was defending evangelical preachers who had an overflow of wit, and who consequently offended some of their more pious brethren. As they apply most of the time, I have taken the liberty of applying Spurgeon's observations to our subject. The striking thing about his book is that there have been so many *sane* preachers laboring in the midst of an insane primness and respectability.

Whenever the Christian faith is accepted and established in a nation, and a large number of people are members of various churches, one of the first and deadliest temptations is the lust

1. Salem: Schmul Publishing Company, 1984 .

for respectability—a lust which is defined and established by complacent worldly values, and not by the Scriptures. Soon the pulpits of the land are filled with a bunch of contented moo cows, and everything settles down into what theologians call bovine ecclesiology. In such a setting, because cows cannot run very fast, it does not take much to pull the tail of the establishment, and God has frequently appointed holy men to this honored and sacred task.

Of course, we are not to defend flip and irreverent insults to the truths of God themselves. As Spurgeon put it, "the man who shocks decency and plays with solemn truths is unworthy of his office."[2] This is very true, but it must be remembered that Spurgeon made this comment in the course of an extended defense of men who were accused of doing precisely that. There is a difference between insulting the truth of God and insulting some lunacy that a televangelist is maintaining as the truth of God. There is a difference between kicking puppies and lampooning the self-righteous and pompous, although sometimes the sound effects are very similar.

In one particularly insightful portion of his book, Spurgeon analyzed why certain effective men were attacked for being "eccentric." Today we would not use the word *eccentric*, preferring instead words like *erratic* or *sarcastic* or *arrogant*. But a review of Spurgeon's comments reveals that basically the same thing was going on. Our vocabulary has changed, but the circumstances have not. And we have a screaming need for what diplomats call a frank "exchange of views." The melodrama

2. Ibid., 42.

of modern evangelicalism has gotten really bad, and it is time to start an enthusiastic throwing of popcorn.

Spurgeon brought forward some basic considerations. "Some ministers have been reckoned eccentric simply and only because *they have been natural.*"[3] We can consider this from two directions. In the first place, such men have simply functioned as God made them. Created with certain gifts (or quirks) of nature and personality, they have simply been themselves. They see the world the way they see it, and nothing can really be done about it.

In the second place, they have not really sought to "do something about it," at least not successfully, and have avoided affectation and a slavish imitation of certain "approved manners."

Cold-hearted professionals follow each other in one line, like those caterpillars which I have seen . . . which make a procession head to tail in a straight line, till you half fancy it is only one single insect; but the man who serves his God with his whole heart is apt to forget his surroundings, and to fling himself so completely into his work that the whole of his nature comes into action, *and even his humour, if he be possessed of that faculty, rushes into the battle.*[4]

The second reason Spurgeon adduced is that some "men have been dubbed eccentric because *they have been more truthful than their fellows.*"[5] We live in a time that is dominated by folly,

3. Ibid., 72.
4. Ibid., 75–76 [emphasis added].
5. Ibid., 76.

and it appears also to be a time when the vast majority of the Christian Church has joined a conspiracy to refrain from telling the truth about the first point. We have all agreed to look the other way. Of course, the truth may be spoken sinfully, in a harsh and ungodly manner. But Spurgeon was exactly right when he said we cannot have too much of the eccentricity of truth speaking "if it be accompanied by sincere affection and tempered with gentleness."[6]

> But of this I feel quite sure, that if any man will make up his mind that he will only say what he believes to be strictly true, he will be thought eccentric before the sun goes down.[7]

The third reason why valuable servants are dismissed as eccentric is because *"they have been manly,* too manly to be hampered by the customs and manners of the period. They have broken through one and another of the rules which have been constructed for the propping up of mannikins, and have behaved themselves as men."[8]

Liturgical rules and confessional customs in every denomination of Christians can rapidly take on the authority of the Scriptures. This is not presented as an argument against liturgy or confessions (for both are inescapable) but rather against a particular mindless conformity to both, which is the death of all true faithfulness. Where this evil rules, Spurgeon wrote, it is assumed that "the preacher must submit to all the regular fudge as if it were Scripture itself."[9]

6. Ibid., 79.
7. Ibid., 79.
8. Ibid., 79–80.
9. Ibid., 81.

A man that *is* a man will yield for peace sake as far as his soul is unhampered, but beyond that he will ask, "Who makes these regulations, and to what end are they made?" Finding them to be worthless and injurious, he will put his foot through them, and there will be an end of the rubbish.[10]

Resistance to a mindless and fastidious approach to the Christian faith is a mark of Christian masculinity. But we live in an effeminate age, one that is far worse in this regard than the times in which Spurgeon lived. This makes application of his insight simultaneously far more difficult *and far more necessary*. Not only are we up against the pietistic foppery that has been present in the Church in every age, we are also up against a prevailing feminism.

This feminism is very dangerous because one wing of it is pervasive in the conservative wing of the Church and is disguised as "traditional values." What many conservative Christians suppose to be the antithesis of contemporary feminism is simply that same feminism in its nineteenth century form. But this is like maintaining that there is an antithesis between being two months pregnant and eight months pregnant.

But the task is most necessary, and the future of the Church is (always) at stake. "Primness, fashionableness, and dignity are but little separated from the ridiculous; at their very best there is but one step between them, and that step is often taken with grave obliviousness that it is so."[11] The modern evangelical church is enamored of her idols—and no idol has ever been toppled without having been made ridiculous first.

10. Ibid., 81–82.
11. Ibid., 84.

When Gideon pulled down the local Baal, that Baal's inability to defend itself was noted by the surrounding residents, and it appeared that they were predisposed to this opinion.

Fourth, Spurgeon noted that "some men have been styled eccentric because *they are really in earnest,* and earnestness defies rules."[12] An earnest man wants to get the work done, and many times the customs of propriety get in the way of getting that work done. It was proper for Peter to work naked in the fishing boat, but not when walking through town. When the work was pressing, Peter apparently felt that his outer clothes got in the way—and getting the work done was paramount.

In the same way, there are occasions when the conventions of polite speech have to come off. But this is done with the accomplishment of the work in view. The right kind of single-mindedness knows what it is after—and goes after it. When the occasion is right, then earnestness demands plain dealing. When the time is not right, then standard proprieties are to be observed. Now some might object that if *this* is the point, then why does *Credenda* maintain a mocking tone throughout its pages? And the answer to this is simple enough: it does not. The majority of the magazine is simply straight prose. The high-jinks are relegated to a just few places, like the "Cave of Adullam," "Cretan Times," or the "Sharpening Iron" section, but for many those places have become a lens through which readers have come to read the whole. This is revealed when people complain that they wish *Credenda* could be more edifying and helpful—like *Reforming Marriage* or *Fruit of Her Hands.*

12. Spurgeon, *Eccentric Preachers,* 84.

But what this misses is that the backbone of those books are columns taken out of *Credenda*.

Fifth, a "few divines have seemed to be eccentric because of the wealth of poetry which dwelt in their speech."[13] Images and figures and humor and metaphor are lost on those who "don't get them." Reading is an active practice, and the writer has to assume certain things on the part of the reader. If they are not there, then a reader who missed the point frequently assumes that the writer is a dullard, when actually the dullness lies elsewhere. As Spurgeon put it, "It needs genius in the hearer to enjoy genius in the preacher."[14] The point is an important one: many times a piece of writing is judged on a very superficial level, and the depths that are there are ignored by readers who resent being challenged.

> Doubtless there are many others who are condemned for their eccentricity by the simpletons around them, because they have wealthy creative minds, and scatter pearls with both their hands.[15]

Sixth, eccentricity "has also been charged on men of shrewd common sense."[16] When a doctrinal scam is being run, men with a little bit of horse sense take it in at a glance and offer some public analysis of the situation. They "leveled a little mother-wit at cants, and hypocrites, and deriders, and so they

13. Ibid., 85.
14. Ibid., 85.
15. Ibid., 86.
16. Ibid., 87.

must be libelled as odd fellows."[17] They are "too honest to be very polite."[18]

In summary, such gadflies in the Church are valuable men. The work available for them to do far exceeds the number of qualified men we have laboring at it. Such men are equipped for the task—they are natural and do not accept the dictates of artificiality. They are honest men, and they are disgusted by lies. This remains the case even if the lies have achieved the status of the currently accepted wisdom and have the support of the staff writers down at *Books and Culture*. Such men are masculine; they have not accepted the dictates of our effeminate times, and, despite all exhortations to the contrary, they have kept their backbone. They are dedicated to the advancement of the kingdom of God. Consequently they are earnest about their work, and they stay at it. As servants of the *Word* of God, they love the exaltation of high poetry and the low rumble-bumble of earthy words. And last, they are shrewd men and know the real nature of the solemn monkeyshines that occur all around them. If asked, they will point them out.

17. Ibid., 87.
18. Ibid., 110.

NINE
Objections

I am not so foolish as to assume there are no counter-arguments. This chapter is intended to answer a few of the more common replies, and to do so in an order that reflects how these arguments frequently run.

The first "argument" is really just an assumed default position—which is that this kind of behavior is self-evidently unbiblical. Since so many agree with this assumption, these advocates rarely need to argue for it, and so when the "offensive" behavior arises it need only be dismissed. But earlier chapters in this book were dedicated to show that far from being a sinful form of expression, the biblical writers frequently employed it themselves and that it is pervasive throughout the scriptural record.

Now if someone were to maintain that saccharine romance stories were necessarily sinful, the defender of such stories would only have to point to the places in the Bible that contain such stories. This would be difficult to do, but that is not my point here. My point is only that if such examples were produced, this would be sufficient to show that the form is not *inherently* sinful. This does not mean that any story that I write in this form will meet the scriptural standard; it merely means that the genre cannot be condemned out of hand. Following this out, it means that satire, both Horatian and Juvenalian, can be a God-honoring form of insult—which has been already demonstrated.

And this leads to the second line of argumentation, which we may sum up with the words—"You're not Jesus, pal." In other words, Jesus can do this because He is the perfect man. The apostles and prophets can do it because they were inspired by the Holy Spirit. We, on the other hand, have no promises or assurances from God that we will be able to do any of this right, and so consequently we had better be safe than sorry. But *safe* by what standard? *Sorry* by what standard?

The problem here is that "the rule" applies equally to everything that Jesus did and all that the apostles and prophets wrote. Since they were perfect or inspired or both, and we are not, then *any* imitation we undertake will necessarily be imperfect. We will be imperfect as we imitate love, grace, forgiveness, kindness, rebuke, sarcasm, gentleness, and so on. Therefore we ought not to strive to be godly at all. We must remain in our ungodliness for fear that an attempt to be godly may result in ungodly failure. This is like refusing to get out of the water because we still might have some wet skin standing there by the side of the pool.

The retort may then come back that we simply need to apply "the rule" to hard-hitting comments, satire, sarcasm, and so forth. But this begs the question: What standard are we

using to say that we should imitate *this* part of Christ's demeanor and refuse to imitate *that* part of it? What standard
do we use to assemble this hierarchy of verbal values? Why
do we say, "Imitate Christ in His kindness to the tax gather-
ers, but *never* imitate Him in His treatment of the religiously
pompous?" Why not the reverse? "*Always* make fun of religious
wowsers, but never imitate Christ's kindness to the downtrod-
den." This kind of selectivity is not approaching the Scriptures as the Word of God but rather belongs to the "scissors
and library paste" school of hermeneutics.

Not surprisingly, this contradicts what we are expressly
told to do. "For I have given you an example, that ye should do
as I have done to you" (Jn. 13:15). Jesus Christ is our perfect
example, our perfect exemplar. "For even hereunto were ye
called: because Christ also suffered for us, *leaving us an example,*
that ye should follow his steps: Who did no sin, neither was
guile found in his mouth" (I Pet. 2:21–22). We are told to
imitate, period. Obviously, in the case of Christ, we are not
being told to imitate His incommunicable divine attributes—
omniscience, and so on. But He is the perfect man; He is what
we are called to grow up into. In His perfect humanity, He is
our elder brother, and we are to look up to Him as younger
brothers and sisters do.

We learn the same principle from Paul.

Brethren, *be followers together of me,* and mark them which
walk *so as ye have us for an ensample.* (For many walk, of
whom I have told you often, and now tell you even weep-
ing, that they are the enemies of the cross of Christ:
Whose end is destruction, whose God is their belly,

and whose glory is in their shame, who mind earthly things.) For our conversation is in heaven; from whence also we look for the Saviour, the Lord Jesus Christ: Who shall change our vile body, that it may be fashioned like unto his glorious body, according to the working whereby he is able even to subdue all things unto himself. (Phil. 3:17–21)

In this passage, Paul plainly tells us that we are to follow his example. Then he tells us that there are those who do not do this—they are enemies of the cross of Christ. And what example is given to us in speaking of such enemies? The first thing Paul says is blunt enough—their end is destruction. But he goes on, and the satiric element comes in—as he puts it, he is against those "whose highest point of worship is the lower gullet." They glory in their shame, rolling around in it. Their mind is on earthly things, like so many pigs under an oak tree looking for acorns. No need to look up.

Imitate *me*, Paul says, and he does not charge us to be arbitrarily selective as we do so. Peter does something similar when he commands elders to be examples for the flock.

The elders which are among you I exhort, who am also an elder, and a witness of the sufferings of Christ, and also a partaker of the glory that shall be revealed: Feed the flock of God which is among you, taking the oversight thereof, not by constraint, but willingly; not for filthy lucre, but of a ready mind; Neither as being lords over God's heritage, *but being ensamples to the flock.* (1 Pet. 5:1–3)

Peter does more than tell the elders to be sweet and nice. He also gives examples of what bad eldering might look like— men who were strong-armed into office, or others who were after "filthy lucre," or men who wanted to be *lords* of *sheep*. *Shepherd* was not an exalted enough title; in a Yertle the Turtle kind of way they insisted on far more.

The pagan approach to moral leadership is always to clamor for "role models." The biblical way is always to take a shot at how it is done wrong, which is what Peter does here. Can we imitate him in this? We are commanded to. Is it lawful to say that a man ought not to go into the ministry because it is an indoor job with no heavy lifting? The particular expression is not required, but the basic approach *is*.

The Scriptures were given to us so that we might shape our lives in accordance with them. This includes our verbal lives. "Take, my brethren, the prophets, who have spoken in the name of the Lord, for an example of suffering affliction, and of patience" (Jas. 5:10). We are to imitate the Lord, and the apostles, but also the prophets of the Old Testament. These prophets were an example in how they suffered affliction, and how they showed an enduring patience. But they did so while *speaking* "in the name of the Lord." Was Jeremiah one of these exemplars? Obviously. Did he mock those who trusted in the wrong thing?

> Trust ye not in lying words, saying, The temple of the LORD, The temple of the LORD, The temple of the LORD, are these. (Jer. 7:4)

This is no skin off our nose because we are not religiously (and idolatrously) attached to a Temple. But what happens if

someone does imitate Jeremiah's patient suffering of affliction while going through some gnat-strangling church trial
in an historic Reformed denomination? And shall we say that
the idol he mentions is something we *are* attached to? "Trust
not in lying words, saying, the BCO! the BCO! the BCO! are
these." All of a sudden everything comes unhinged, and long-
faced litigious types start to *tut tut* through their sinuses.

This requirement that we set examples and follow them is
intended as an on going standard. Paul tells Timothy to carry
this pattern on. He in turn was to instruct others so that they
could do the same (2 Tim. 2:2). And part of what he required
of Timothy was this:

> Let no man despise thy youth; *but be thou an example* of
> the believers, in *word*, in *conversation*, in charity, in spirit,
> in faith, in purity. (I Tim. 4:12, emphasis mine)

By this point, some readers may be exasperated. "*See?* It says
'word, conversation, *charity*.'" There will be more on this in the
last chapter, but the basic problem concerns what we mean by
charity. What is love? Love is doing what God says to do, the
way He says to do it, with a whole heart.

And this leads to the last point, and what is perhaps the
real reason for much of the concern about this subject. Many
who object to satire as a godly weapon of war have this preju-
dice against it because they grew up in a home where sarcasm
was consistently used as an ungodly bludgeoning tool. Just
as a child who grows up in a home where both parents have
a problem with drunkenness will likely have a problem with
godly and biblical drinking, so a wounded child—wounded
by an acidic parental tongue—will likely have a problem with

Christians using satire. This is the case even when the objects of the satire are not helpless children but those who are making the holy things of God a laughingstock. This is the kind of problem with association that does not readily admit of logical calculus. A child of alcoholics may watch a Christian drink responsibly for thirty years and yet still be afraid of the potential for drunkenness. There are many Christians who wince at any satire because of how they have seen it employed. Mark Twain once said that a cat that sits on a hot stove lid will never sit on a hot stove again. Neither will it sit on a cold one.

The response to this—which has to be made with kindness—is that the Bible is our standard, and not our personal histories. We may empathize with those who feel this way (and we do), but we must not abandon our commitment to biblical living on the basis of it. The Bible tells us to receive weaker brothers, but not in order to dispute with them. And indeed, our dispute has never been with them.

TEN
The Goal of Giving Offense

Few subjects are as badly neglected in the modern Church as the applied field of biblical polemics. As a result, we have done very little thinking on the goal of this kind of satire in controversy. Of course, the point of everything is to glorify God, but how does satire glorify God?

Because we have not thought through this, our default assumption is that if anyone is engaged in polemical or satiric activity, it must be the result of the polemicist having a thin skin, and this is thought to be what has brought on the theological hissy fit. The picture is complicated by the fact that this judgment frequently is accurate, particularly when it comes to debates on the Internet. Someone melts down in a blaze of invective, earning three jalapeno icons from his email program and the pity of all Spirit-filled onlookers. This really is a problem, but we still have to be careful. All cows have four legs, but not all cats are cows. All invective-spewing melt-downers use sarcasm, but that tells us nothing about a godly use of satire.

Because we have not studied this properly, when controversy breaks out in the modern Church it is therefore likely that all parties to the controversy share certain assumptions about what is appropriate in conflict and what is not, and these hidden assumptions tend to govern their discourse instead of the example and pattern of Scripture. We look at the debates of the Reformation era with stunned disbelief, and the way Athanasius treated his opponents was not much better. Our sentimentalist assumptions cause us to assume that the rough and tumble of polemical discourse is automatically out of line and pointless. But if we look to Scripture, we see that there is a point.

I want to argue that this hidden compromise of method vitiates the attempts of those believers who attempt to be faithful to the content of Scripture, as well as to the content of their confessional heritage. Simply presenting the truth of God in a computer printout fashion, without the passion, life, satire, love, and emotion found in Scripture, is a way of being unfaithful to that content. Style is far more than the simple decoration of propositions. Style (with satire as an important part of this) should be woven throughout every discourse and considered an essential part of it. Because we have pursued an "objective" style of communication (having believed that this was possible), we have created a deracinated and boring form of speech. We have confused agape love with blah. We are like soldiers who blunt their swords before they go into battle, believing that this is all right if we ensure that the swords still weigh what they used to. The content is still there.

Of course, it has to be emphasized that in a particular kind of religious controversy the central point is to accomplish reconciliation, and that to fail in this task is to fail in maintaining the spirit of unity in the bond of peace. The Scriptures address this in multiple places. We are to put on tender mercies. We are to love one another. We are to bear with one another, and this does not include unloading a verbal dump truck on your brothers and sisters. The Bible speaks of this in many places, and, for the most part, we are aware of this teaching. It is not practiced as it should be, but at least its existence is not ignored.

With all lowliness and meekness, with longsuffering, forbearing one another in love; endeavouring to keep the unity of the Spirit in the bond of peace. There is one body, and one Spirit, even as ye are called in one hope of your calling; one Lord, one faith, one baptism, one God and Father of all, who is above all, and through all, and in you all. (Eph. 4:2–6)

Because God is one, we are to be one. He has made this clear to us by giving us a baptism which reflects His triune glory. We are therefore to receive one another but not into disputes about debatable things. The Church of God is not a society created by God so that we might devote ourselves to quarreling. Spitting at one another is out.

At the same time, precisely because the Church is the household of the faithful, the enemy outside hates it. One of the ways he expresses that hatred is by various attempts at subversion, corrupting the Church from within. It is simply naive to maintain that all assaults on the faith come from persecuting tyrants. Most of the threats to biblical integrity come from men who went to seminary. The beast in Scripture is a civil ruler, persecuting from outside. There have been many such beasts in the history of the Church, from Nero to Stalin. But the antichrist in Scripture is a spirit of corruption from within the body. Who is the antichrist but the one who denies that Jesus came in the flesh? (I Jn. 4:3). A beast is a persecutor; an antichrist is a false teacher. In the scriptural categories, Hitler was a beast, but to find our modern antichrists we have to look for liberal Methodist bishops and the lesbians who love them. Now the Bible requires that the Word be brought against both kinds of threats, which is just what the apostle John did. He brought the Word against the beast in Revelation and against the antichrist in I John. And when that Word comes, it does not do so as an invitation to dialogue.

Now if I were to say that there ought to be no fighting around the dinner table in a Christian home, I trust that everyone would know what I meant. And if they really understood this, they would be ready to allow for legitimate exceptions—say, if a bear got into the house. If a husband were to fight under such circumstances, he would not be abusing the principle of "peace around the dinner table." The principle is not peace-at-any-price around the dinner table.

This means, following the many examples of Scripture, that there is a different kind of religious controversy, where the central point is to give offense. Failure in such controversy would be reckoned as a failure to give offense in the way Scripture requires, and for the reasons given in Scripture. We determine when and how to enter into such a fracas through careful Bible study. And one of the things we discover there is that Scripture demands that we seek to offend willful obstinacy by ecclesiastical officials in the face of the grace of God. Failure to distinguish these two kinds of controversy, or a flat denial that there is ever a time when giving offense is a spiritual obligation, means in effect, that in the great basketball game between obedience and disobedience, the referees are always on the take. We are not left to our own devices in figuring this out. Our Lord Jesus, when confronted with ecclesiastical obstinacy, showed us this godly pattern for giving offense.

> And he called the multitude, and said unto them, Hear, and understand: Not that which goeth into the mouth defileth a man; but that which cometh out of the mouth, this defileth a man. Then came his disciples, and said unto him, Knowest thou that the Pharisees were offended, after they heard this saying? But he answered and said, Every plant, which my heavenly Father hath not planted, shall be rooted up. Let them alone: they be blind leaders of the blind. And if the blind lead the blind, both shall fall into the ditch. (Mt. 15:10–14)

The disciples were worried about the effects of the Lord's rhetoric. Did you know the Pharisees were offended when they heard this? (Mt. 15:12). Yes, I did, He replied in effect. His mission was accomplished (v. 13). The Lord attacked the scribes and Pharisees for their long robes, sanctimonious geegaws, prayer habits, tithing practices, their ways of greeting, their seating arrangements, their hypocrisies, and so on. If the Pharisees had funny hairdos, like they do on TBN, we would have heard about that too.

But woe unto you, Pharisees! for ye tithe mint and rue
and all manner of herbs, and pass over judgment and
the love of God: these ought ye to have done, and not
to leave the other undone. Woe unto you, Pharisees!
for ye love the uppermost seats in the synagogues, and
greetings in the markets. Woe unto you, scribes and
Pharisees, hypocrites! for ye are as graves which appear
not, and the men that walk over them are not aware
of them. Then answered one of the lawyers, and said
unto him, Master, thus saying thou reproachest us
also. And he said, Woe unto you also, ye lawyers! for
ye lade men with burdens grievous to be borne, and
ye yourselves touch not the burdens with one of your
fingers. (Lk. 11:42–46)

Notice that this passage shows a by-standing lawyer men-
tioning that Jesus was insulting them in His indictment too
(v. 45). And in effect Jesus said, "Oh, yes, thanks for that
reminder. You lawyers . . ." (v. 46). In short, Jesus was seeking to offend.

This is inescapable. In a sinful world, giving offense is one
of the central tasks of preaching. When the offending word is
brought to bear against those who have shown themselves to be
unteachable, they are written off by that offending word. When
this happens, or there is a threat of it happening, the natural
temptation is to blame the word instead of taking responsi-
bility for the sin that brought the rebuking and satiric word.
Employing a scriptural satiric bite is therefore not "rejoicing in
iniquity" but rather testifying against hardness of heart.

This is why, in every controversy, godliness and wisdom (or
the lack of them) are to be determined by careful appeal to

the Scriptures and not to the fact of someone having taken offense. Perhaps they ought to have taken offense, and perhaps someone ought to have endeavored to give it.

But this is not a one-size-fits-all approach. Sometimes a fool is not to be answered according to his folly. "Answer not a fool according to his folly, lest thou also be like unto him" (Prov. 26:4). The reason given is that there is a temptation for the satiric attacker of folly to become a fool himself. Don't stoop to his level because you might find it hard to get up.

This is why the Bible teaches that those who contradict are to be answered in all gentleness.

> But foolish and unlearned questions avoid, knowing that they do gender strifes. And the servant of the Lord must not strive; but be gentle unto all men, apt to teach, patient, in meekness instructing those that oppose themselves; if God peradventure will give them repentance to the acknowledging of the truth; and that they may recover themselves out of the snare of the devil, who are taken captive by him at his will. (2 Tim. 2:23–25)

This instruction must be embraced and practiced, but it must be embraced and practiced in all wisdom. This is because in other situations a fool must be answered according to his folly lest he become wise in his own conceits. "Answer a fool according to his folly, lest he be wise in his own conceit" (Prov. 26:5). In other words, the Bible says that answering a fool does provide a temptation to the satirist, and so he must watch out. But not answering provides a temptation to the fool and allows him to marinate further in the juices of his own vainglory. This is why those who oppose the truth are to be rebuked sharply.

One of themselves, even a prophet of their own, said, The Cretans are always liars, evil beasts, slow bellies. This witness is true. Wherefore rebuke them sharply, that they may be sound in the faith; not giving heed to Jewish fables, and commandments of men, that turn from the truth. (Tit. 1:12–14)

When rebukes are delivered, it should be done with all authority. "These things speak, and exhort, and rebuke with all authority. Let no man despise thee" (Tit. 2:15). Such admonitions, exhortations, and jabs are to be delivered with love for God, love for His Word, love for His Church, and a zeal to be faithful. Because faithfulness in this kind of prophetic utterance is measured by Scripture, we cannot evaluate these things like the disciples did, bustling up to Jesus to let him know the Pharisees were offended. Of course they were offended. Who knows how God will use such words? His Word does not return void. Perhaps the hard-hearted hypocrite will not be able to shake the rebuke and will come to true faith a decade later. Perhaps he never will. But then someone outside the faith who believed that the Christian faith was bogus—because of all the tolerated hypocrisy—might come to hear of the attack and repent and believe.

When we find examples in Scripture (and in Church history) of men who can do both—comfort the afflicted and afflict the comfortable—we have to take care that we categorize them as the Bible teaches us to. They are not to be thought of as conflicted personalities, but rather as examples of obedience and balance.

Of course, in saying all this, there are a few caveats of the "don't try this at home" variety. I believe that true biblical balance in such things is the fruit of wisdom, and that such balance is not usually found in hot-headed young men who do not know what spirit they are of (Lk. 9:55). Consequently, prophetic rebukes should come from seasoned prophets, from men called to the ministry of guarding those people who belong to the Lord. The work should be done by men of some age and wisdom, and not by novices, firebrands, and zealots. The work should most certainly not be done by the kind of man who practices on his mom, wife, or kids. Satire is a weapon to be employed in the warfare of the kingdom, not an opportunity for personal venting. A man who has a *need* to cut others is a man who ought to be silent.

Certainly the Lord Jesus Christ is always to be our example in dealing with certain kinds of religious leaders, and where He has set an example, we must strive to follow Him. But part of this means we must be careful not to be *hasty* in imitating Him, since His wisdom is perfect and ours is not. It is therefore good to take counsel with others. Related to this, sharp rebukes and the ridiculing of evil practices should seldom be the first approach one should make, but usually should follow only after the rejection of a soft word of reproach, or when dealing with hard-hearted obstinacy displayed over an extended period of time. If this is not remembered the satirist will find himself killing ants with a baseball bat.

And of course, we must be careful not to let strong language and supposedly righteous anger be a substitute for good arguments to be employed whenever we feel threatened. Strong language must be weighed and measured and must always have a point.

ELEVEN
Apathetic Sanctity

The use of satire and pointed humor in *Credenda* is usually located in one of four places—our feature called the "Cave of Adullam," our letters section entitled "Sharpening Iron," our fake news stories in "Cretan Times," and comments located in the masthead.

There are also comments here and there in some of the columns that I write which can be counted as satiric, but they do not really establish the tone of the magazine. This should be clear from the fact that many of those who complain or comment about the tone of *Credenda*, as mentioned earlier, often express a follow-up wish that the magazine could be more like the books that Canon Press publishes on the family and child-rearing. But the bulk of the material for these books had its first appearance in *Credenda*. In other words, it is very likely that the comments in the three sections I mentioned above (which constitute a small percentage of the magazine) color the perception that people have of the whole magazine. And so when material from elsewhere in the magazine appears in uncontaminated containers, it is far more likely to be seen for what it is.

A key link between all these features is hopefully a sanctified apathy. The word *apathy* has all kinds of negative connotations, and rightly so. But I would like to commend the word for at least one positive application if for no other reason than to make us think about how we interact with the culture around us. The word means to "not care," but it also carries the sense that the reason for not caring is lethargy, pride, or some other character failing. When Sosthenes was beat up outside the place of judgment, the judge, a man named Gallio, cared for none of these things (Acts 18:17). Gallio was the brother of Seneca, the famous Stoic philosopher, and the Stoics were famous for not caring about things. Maybe Gallio had picked up a few tips.

But there is a godly way of not caring. When Shadrach, Meshach, and Abednego were commanded to bow down to the Babylonian idol, they refused. They knew that God was able to deliver them, and they said as much to the king. "If it be so, our God whom we serve is able to deliver us from the burning fiery furnace, and he will deliver us out of thine hand, O king. But if not, be it known unto thee, O king, that we will not serve thy gods, nor worship the golden image which thou hast set up" (Dan. 3:17–18). They said that their God could deliver them. But even if He decided not to, as far as they were concerned, the king could throw them into the furnace. They didn't care. Of course they didn't care about the furnace because they did care, and deeply, about honoring God. And this is the basis for sanctified apathy.

The more we care about honoring God, the less we will care about receiving honors from men. This is important because if we care about the opinions of men in the wrong way, it keeps us from being able to believe (Jn. 5:44). The more we care about being approved as faithful workmen by God, the less we will care if others condemn or oppose us on their own puny authority (2 Tim. 2:15).

Modern Christians are constantly exhorted to care. This is legitimate, indeed it is inescapable. But the problem is that we are regularly told to care about all the wrong things. "If we continue to maintain that God created the world in six days, we will not be granted academic respectability." To which we must reply, well, who cares? Why should we care that the guardians of the academy believe that *we* are not intellectually respectable? They believe that the moose, the sperm whale and the meadowlark are all blood relations. Why do we want their seal of approval on our intellectual abilities? It is like asking Fidel Castro to comment on the economic viability of Microsoft.

But there is another twist. Pragmatic calculations are frequently self-defeating. The man who buries his talent in the ground, after a very careful risk analysis, is the man rebuked by his "hard" master. The man desperate for respect is often the one who receiveth it not, while the one who strives for excellence as defined by God in heaven—he stands before kings (Prov. 22:29). In the kingdom of God, the one who would be great must become the least of all. The one who would rule must serve. The one who wants praise must not care about praise.

However, we are created to need praise. So the only choice we have is whether that need will be expressed vertically (Godward) or horizontally (manward). Will we seek to hear, "well done, good and faithful servant"? Or are our lives lived for the attaboy?

We are also told that we are seeking praise from the place where we offer praise. Those who seek praise from men always prime the pump by offering their own praise first, and we call this flattery. Those who seek praise from God are those who give the glory, all of it, to the Lord. "But he that glorieth, let him glory in the Lord. For not he that commendeth himself is approved, but whom the Lord commendeth" (2 Cor. 10:17–18). We are told to render glory to God, and, in return, we are commended by Him. But if we commend ourselves, we are not approved by God, however much we feel our self-esteem may have been enhanced.

The meek inherit the earth. Meekness is submission before God, and those who bow before God alone are told that they are kings and priests on the earth. The idolatrously insecure will inherit nothing. And when nothing is experienced but the outer darkness, there will be no echoes of flattering praise at all.

Living this way, before the face of God, keeps our "not caring" from being a self-contained arrogance. Some people don't care about what other people think for all the wrong reasons. They do not acknowledge the idols in the neighboring city because they are enamored of their own idols. But humility before God means that humility extends all the way out to the periphery of our lives. At the same time, the authority of the living God extends this far as well. So we certainly do not want to make ourselves obnoxious to men just for the sake of doing so. Christians are not called to cultivate bad breath, bad manners, and so on. As far as it is possible with us, we should be at peace with all men. But the priorities have to be right. "For he that in these things serveth Christ is acceptable to God, and approved of men" (Rom. 14:18).

TWELVE
Tender Mercies

There is no real way to keep an *apologia* like this from addressing, however obliquely, the fact that we are doing something
we believe to be defensible, and that we are doing it in a *way*
that we believe admirable. Otherwise, if we did not believe
this, we should shut up and repent.

This approach is awkward under any circumstances, but is
easier to do when defending oneself against a charge of sin.
When that is the case, the burden of proof is on the accuser
anyway, and it is not as difficult to avoid being a pompous
windbag when defending yourself.

The hard part comes when discussing what most Christians agree are positive virtues. When the apostle Paul was
provoked into this kind of discussion, he resorted to a typi-
cally Pauline disclaimer, which was that he was out of his
mind to talk this way (1 Cor. 3:20). The one who boasts
should boast in the Lord (2 Cor. 10:17), and no one of us
has anything that is not a gift from God (1 Cor. 4:7). And

if it is a gift, then how can we boast as though it is not? This said, let me echo Paul's disclaimer. I would not talk this way unless it was an essential part of the defense. Paul taught us that it is appropriate for a minister to defend his character to the extent that the defense of the ministry depends upon it. At the same time, I don't like it, and mean to keep it brief.

A common argument against the satiric approach is that it is counterproductive; it turns people off. The problem with this argument is that it is simply not true. A certain kind of person is turned off, that is true enough, but another kind of person is attracted to the ministry because of it and flourishes there. During the time that we have been ministering in this way (for many years now), God has consistently blessed the work of our hands, in countless ways. The warning that what we are doing is turning people way comes to us at a time when we see a wonderful gathering of people, churches, ministries, all of them a blessing.

The blessing has been so significant that we have continued our satiric tact with an additional objective in mind—keeping the suits and haircuts away. Whenever a promising movement of the Holy Spirit begins nowadays, one of the first things that happens is that the agents, businessmen, and other assorted handlers move in so that they might straighten out certain unmarketable "blemishes" in order to take the show on the road. And when a promising ministry hits the big time, the unfortunate people in it are made twice as much sons of hell as their promoters. It is therefore our resolve to stay as unmarketable as we can. If we ever get invited to the Great Black Tie Banquet of Evangelicalism, we want everyone there to be braced for the moment when we, on a prearranged signal, throw our dinner rolls at Pat Robertson. Thus far this strategy appears to have worked and has thinned out the invitations. This, in our view, is not a bad thing. We are not quenching the Spirit. We want spiritual words—which have that serrated edge—to quench the gospel-mongers.

In the meantime, as God calls us to live together, we are summoned to live in a certain way.

> Put on therefore, as the elect of God, holy and beloved, bowels of mercies, kindness, humbleness of mind, meekness, longsuffering; forbearing one another, and forgiving one another, if any man have a quarrel against any: even as Christ forgave you, so also do ye. (Col. 3:12–13)

The men I work with, who are satirically gifted, and who employ those gifts on appropriate targets, are men who are tender and compassionate—in the *scriptural* sense described above. At the time of writing, the offices of Christ Church, Canon Press, *Credenda*, and New St. Andrews all share a common location, and have done so for years. During those years, there has not been one quarrel or fight in these offices. The people who work in these ministries are characterized by a spirit of mutual submission, and the dominant and ongoing tone in the offices is one of laughter, peace, joy, and *kindness*. The same kind of kindness and joy is pervasive in the church where I am privileged to serve as a pastor.

We have been rebuked by people who believe we are unloving and that the motives of our hearts are corrupt. This kind of charge usually comes from people who do not know us at all—what I call Great Experiments in Telepathy. Sometimes it comes from those who do know us, but a general inconsistency is apparent here as well. We are familiar with the temptation. It goes back to Linus of *Peanuts* fame. "I love mankind, it's people I can't stand." Or, as P. J. O'Rourke put it somewhere, "Everyone wants to save the world, but no one wants to help mom with the dishes." The inconsistency comes out in two ways. One is in the type of person who thinks we ought to be more loving in our polemical discourse. They do not appreciate what we have to say about the follies of modern evangelicalism—but they themselves are mocking of those who are close to them. In other words, it is a sin to make fun of God-dishonoring activity at Willow Creek but not a problem to make fun of your own six-year-old daughter. The problem here is obvious. The second problem is that of the dour pietist. He does not mock his own friends and family but rather is simply joyless across the board. He wants to see more grief over the unbelief of our day. In fact, this prunish grief is so important that one must practice it all the time— at dinner, in worship, at his kid's birthday party, and so on. Pietistic Calvinists are particularly good at this.

Over against such inconsistent objections, we want to love. We love one another, and we seek to live this way. But does not the Bible say that we are to love our enemies, and pray for those who persecute us? Yes, it does, and yes, we do. But love is defined by *God* and not by Hallmark cards.

Thus far, I have only spoken about those who labor with me in this ministry. But because the tone of *my* writing is a big part of why objections are raised, let me end this short book on a more personal (and serious) note. The argumentation has already been laid out. But there is an autobiographical element in this that I should explain to everyone who has ever wondered about the tone of my writing—where does that *edge* come from? What got under *his* skin?

If you think I have faults, you are certainly right, and I can assure you that it is probably far worse than you think. But shoplifting is not one of them, and neither is nastiness. I am a sinner, but happily my critics at a distance have collectively decided to leave all my real problems alone.

The motivation for all that they do criticize is love. Love that refuses to defend that which is loved is not biblical love at all. Such a sentiment is actually self-absorbtion. Love that shuns a fight is an oxymoron, and so I turn the charge around. The modern evangelical world says peace, peace, but there is no peace. Neither is there love.

I love the right worship of our triune God, the God and Father of the Lord Jesus Christ, and the Holy Spirit of both. I love the Church, despite the make-up she is currently using. I love the Scriptures, and the message of free grace it brings to a race steeped in idolatrous folly. I love my wife, children, and grandchildren. Though I haven't seen them, I love my great-grandchildren and want my descendents to have a place to live in this world where they can worship God with more than three chords. I love my parents, brothers, sister, cousins, nieces, and nephews. God has given us a heritage that I intend to love fiercely until I die. I love the Reformed faith—both its glorious past and yet more glorious future.

And if this serious note makes some readers uncomfortable—though every word of it is true—I also love Pinot Noir, Mozart, Creedence Clearwater Revival, oatmeal stout, Brown Cow ice cream, mowing a field, playing softball, listening to blues, reading with my wife, playing the guitar, P. G. Wode-house, clouds on the mountain, anapestic poetry, and making fun of uncircumcised Philistines.

APPENDIX

Seductive Disrespect

by Douglas Jones

Bravery softens. In an essay discussing some of the means of softening human hearts, Montaigne cites Edward the Black Prince's infamous slaughter of French rebels at Limoges in 1370: "The lamentations of the townsfolk, the women and children left behind to be butchered, crying for mercy and throwing themselves at his feet, did not stop him until eventually, passing ever deeper into the town, he noticed three French noblemen who, alone, with unbelievable bravery, were resisting the thrust of his victorious army. Deference and respect for such remarkable valor first blunted the edge of his anger; then starting with those three he showed mercy on all the other inhabitants of the town."

This episode pictures a wonderful aspect of the Church's interaction with an opposing, dominant culture. Opponents can respect bravery; opponents can be seduced with bravery;

they can be seduced by disrespect. The three French noblemen desperately fighting off Edward's troops were not trying
to gain a place at the table or earn academic respectability or
even be liked. At that moment, they wanted to decapitate and
disembowel every Englishman within the arc of their swords,
including Edward himself if he would just come close enough.
And yet, contrary to all common sense, their bravery, their
disrespect, seduced their attacker.

Christ Himself had a reputation like that of these nobles.
The Pharisees openly recognized and feared that "You are
true, and care about no one; for You do not regard the person
of men, but teach the way of God in truth" (Mk. 12:14, NKJV).
He didn't care about their opinions. He had a reputation of
refusing to kiss up to the cultural elites. In fact, he regularly
mocked them. And this brave faithfulness was perceived as
"authority" (not bravado)—"the people were astonished at His
teaching, for He taught them as one having authority, and
not as the scribes" (Mt. 7:28–29). His disrespect of the surrounding idolatries produced fear and conflict and ultimately
seduced the whole Mediterranean.

It is no surprise that Christ walked in paths already laid by
Elijah, for Elijah was one of the premier proponents of con-
quering via disrespect. He was slandered as that "Troubler of
Israel" (I Kgs. 18:17) even before he publicly humiliated the
priests and idols of his day. And what a scene that was: Elijah
mocking the most prestigious cultural elites, full of idolatrous
seriousness and respectability and middle class decency—
"Elijah mocked them and said, 'Cry aloud, for he is a god;
either he is meditating, or he is busy, or he is on a journey, or
perhaps he is sleeping and must be awakened'" (I Kgs. 18:27).

Elijah proves that the act of mocking arrogance grows out of the Fruit of the Spirit, grows out of true humility. God snatched Elijah to heaven in a whirlwind because He loved him so much.

In our own day, we haven't even waded into the shallows in mocking Modernist arrogance. The biggest opponents to this sort of tactic are most often Christians with deep sentimental streaks who view any ugliness as contrary to the Fruit of the Spirit. How many of us would be embarrassed if "weirdos" like Elijah or John the Baptist showed up in our communities saying the sorts of things they said? Evangelicals would be the first ones to pronounce them Troublers of American Decency.

But mocking arrogance—violating the tyrannical decencies of a prevailing idolatry—has to be only part of the battle. We can't do without out it, but it can't sustain itself either. It's a glorious, sometimes hilarious, negativity, but it has to ride on a deeper, constructive seduction of truth, beauty, and goodness. We can't just tear down Modernity with bravado and then offer cheap immaturity in its place. Imagine Modernity falling, and we're right there to hand them a copy of *The Prayer of Jabez* or even a tome of systematic theology. Those things aren't life. They're just pages of words. And that's pretty much the sum of evangelical culture these days—plenty of words, no actual biblical living. Plenty of magazines, books, and schools—words, words, words—but no mature communities. No wonder God won't bless our evangelism. We don't know how to live any better than Modernists.

In the future, when we do learn better, when we do learn that life on earth is not just to growl around longing to escape earth, that the gospel is primarily concerned with living well now (Eccl. 9:7–9), not resenting life, then we'll truly see the Church seduce the world. God promises it: "for this is your wisdom and your understanding in the sight of the peoples who will hear all these statutes, and say, 'Surely this great nation is a wise and understanding people'" (Deut. 4:6). Pagans are supposed to be wowed by our communities, like Sheba for Solomon: "when the queen of Sheba had seen all the wisdom of Solomon, the house that he had built, the food on his table, the seating of his servants, the service of his waiters and their apparel, his cupbearers, and his entryway by which he went up to the house of the LORD, there was no more spirit in her" (1 Kgs. 10:4–5). No more spirit in her! What a grand description. That's what awaits Modernity. And she confessed, "Blessed be the LORD your God, who delighted in you, setting you on the throne of Israel! Because the LORD has loved Israel forever, therefore He made you king, to do justice and righteousness" (1 Kgs. 10:9).

The Church is called to be a holy seductress. We tend to get tripped up in the negative connotations of seduction and leave the notion to the nasty side. But God Himself is the premier seducer: "Do you despise the riches of His goodness, forbearance, and longsuffering, not knowing that the goodness of God leads you to repentance?" (Rom. 2:4). When drawing Israel to Himself He gave her embroidered cloth, sandals, fine linen, silk, bracelets, necklaces, earrings, and a beautiful crown, and her "fame went out among the nations" because of her beauty, "for it was perfect through My splendor which I had bestowed" on her (Ezek. 16:10–14).

In our latent Gnosticism, we tend to despise the centrality of beauty and goodness in our countercultural battles. We're so busy boycotting or teaching against pagan worldviews that we have little time actually to create anything ourselves—"always learning and never able to come to the knowledge of the truth" (2 Tim. 3:7)—always teaching, never actually living.

We ignore Solomon's successes because of his end. What we really need, then, is a vision that combines the best of Solomon with the best of Elijah—a seductive disrespect that is both negative and positive. The latter is, of course, much more difficult and will take generations. But its glory is that everyone is involved in creating beautiful communities, from the least to the greatest. Different parts of the body creating different things, some swinging at the idols, more showing hospitality, creativity, and robust laughter. Then, as the Black Prince of Modernity continues to lash out in all his unimaginative pettiness, we're there fighting nobly, seducing beautifully. And he will marvel at Christ's Church in all her splendor—"And the nations of those who are saved shall walk in its light, and the kings of the earth bring their glory and honor into it" (Rev. 21:24).

Douglas Jones is senior editor of Credenda/Agenda *magazine.*

SCRIPTURE INDEX

Genesis
3:4 27
29:25 58

Deuteronomy
4:6 124

Judges
3:15 54
3:16 54
3:17 54
3:18 55
3:19–20 55
3:20 55
3:23 55
3:24 55
3:25 55
3:26–30 55

Ruth
3:8–9 58

1 Samuel
25:25 57

2 Samuel
3:29 57

1 Kings
10:4–5 124
10:9 124
18:17 122
18:25–29 53
18:27 122

Job
12:1–2 51
38:1–5 51
40:1–5 52

Psalms
1 59
104:16 47

Proverbs
11:22 14, 49
19:13 50
19:24 49
22:13 49
22:29 113
26:4 59, 107
26:5 59, 107
26:14 49
26:17 49
27:14 49
27:15 50

Ecclesiastes
9:7–9 124
10:1 80
10:8–11 50
10:15 50

Isaiah
3:16–26 14
5:20 16, 24
44:12 55
44:15 56
44:16–17 56
44:18 56
44:20 56
64:6 65

Jeremiah
7:4 97

Ezekiel
16:10–14 124
23:19–21 65

Daniel
3:17–18 112

Amos
4:1 15
6:1–6 48

Matthew
6:2 43
6:5 43
6:16 43
6:34 44
7:1–6 32
7:16 34
7:28–29 122
8:22 34
11:16–19 44
15:10–14 105
15:12 105
15:13 105
15:14 32
15:22–28 45
16:16–18 30
18 67
18:28 34
19:23 31
23 15, 35
23:1–4 35
23:5–6 36

23:7–12 37
23:13 37
23:14 37
23:15 38
23:16–22 38
23:23–28 39
23:29–32 40
23:33 12
23:34–39 42

Mark
4:21 34
7:9–13 42
7:27 45
10:25 31
12:14 122

Luke
6:39 32
6:41 32
6:44 34
7:31–35 44
9:55 109
9:55–56 25
9:60 34
11:39 39
11:42–46 106
11:45 106
11:46 106
11:52 37
13:31–32 30
13:33 30
18:25 31

John
3:16 70
5:44 113
10:32 30
13:15 95

Acts
17:21 14
18:17 14, 112
19:34 14
22:23 15

Romans
2:4 124
14:18 114

1 Corinthians
3:20 115
4:7 115

2 Corinthians
4:5 23
10:12 71
10:17 115
10:17–18 114
11:5–15 33

Galatians
2:11 67
5:11–12 63
5:12 64
5:13 63, 64
5:13–15 64
5:14 64
5:15 64

Ephesians
4:2–6 103
4:31–32 61
5:4 65

Philippians
3:1 64
3:2 64
3:4–7 64

3:8 64
3:17–21 96

Colossians
3:12–13 117
4:6 63

1 Timothy
1:18–20 66
4:12 33, 98

2 Timothy
2:2 98
2:15 113
2:23–25 107
3:7 125
4:14 66

Titus
1:12–14 108
2:15 33, 108

James
5:10 97

1 Peter
2:21–22 95
4:17 80
5:1–3 96

1 John
1:9 61
4:3 104

Revelation
21:24 125